Project
GENIUS
BIG Learning for Young Geniuses

Karen Tui Boyes

"The genius of Karen Boyes shines through in this highly practical book. The concept of Genius Hour supports the best contemporary educational thinking, and especially with project-based learning and student-centred initiatives. If you're serious about implementing a Genius Hour process, this book will be your perfect resource."

– **Tony Ryan.** *Educator, Innovator & Author*

This book provides a road map for what to do with a classroom full of eager, innovative students – also known as "geniuses". Karen captures the delicate balance between tight enough structure for comfort and loose enough opportunities for creativity. This is a fresh contribution to the field of project based learning. I know this book will inspire those who are just getting started as well as offer new insights to those who have been doing this work for years.

– **Dr Bena Kallick.**
Co-Founder and Co-Director, Institute for Habits of Mind

This practical, easy to follow guide is an essential tool for anyone looking to explore a truly revolutionary idea in teaching and learning. It is packed with practical strategies and techniques that can be put into use immediately, either individually or as a complete package. I loved reading it and found myself getting energised all over again as if I was once again a new teacher!

– **Dr. Rich Allen.** *Educator, Author and Master Trainer*

Karen Boyes, a champion for deep learning for all learners, has done it again! This book is a clear guide to anyone wanting to step into project based/genius hour learning opportunities. It is easy to read and easy to follow whilst being full of practical ideas that can enhance your classroom practise. Questions are answered, advice is given and the inspiration is huge.

– **Megan Gallagher.** *Teacher, Leader, Learner*

This valuable book provides a step-by-step handbook for teachers who wish to teach their students how to plan, organise, and present project-based learning. And more than that, as they are working, students transcend the project to also learn the 21st century skills of collaboration, creativity, communication and critical thinking. These are the learnings that they will use not only in school but also as they confront complex problems in their future world.

– **Arthur L Costa, Ed.D.**
Professor Emeritus, California State University Sacramento

Karen Tui Boyes takes her brilliant interpersonal know-how and conveys it through this Genius Hour Project-Based Learning book so that any teacher can be as successful. These methods are the keys to helping young people enjoy learning and create a bright future based on their ability to get wonderful things done in class and in the world.

– **Carol Carter.** *Founder and CEO of Global MindED*

"In a time when it is becoming harder to engage and 'spark a passion for learning' in students, Karen's approach to Genius Hour offers an opportunity to hook in our learners. Starting from exploring their passion then allowing them to apply their knowledge and skills in real life contexts means we are setting them up for an ever-changing future".

– **Michelle Boyde.** *Secondary Teacher*

In this beautifully structured guide to successfully implementing Genius Hour, Karen Tui Boyes provides practical guidance, tools and tips for educators. This great book is a 'must read' for educators who want to implement Genius Hour in their classroom.

– **Steve Francis.** *Educator & Creator of the Happy School Program*

What a great read, in fact, I finished the book in one sitting! I found Project Genius a refreshing and inspiring reminder of what learning should be about; exploration, joy, engagement, zest, stretching and growth. Karen explained this innovative concept of students (and ourselves) delving into areas which they are truly interested, in an engaging and informative way. What a wonderful way to get our young people looking at things in a mindful, curious and questioning way.

– **Mick Walsh.** *Author, Educator and Speaker*

Karen is a true example of what it means to strive for success in our fast paced, ever changing modern world. Her dedication to making a difference for teachers and learners everywhere is once again evident in this book designed for Genius hour. While the clear focus on processes and strategies for teachers and students provides a purposeful guide for Genius Hour projects everywhere it has great relevance for any project based inquiry setting.

– **Chic Foote.** *Curriculum Facilitator*

As educators we are constantly striving for ways to engage students and what better way than to give students the opportunity to deepen their learning about things for which they are passionate. In Project Genius Karen brings together a myriad or ideas, strategies, and stories from real teachers, which will assist educators to implement authentic contexts for learning, linked to the passion of their students. This book will be a useful guide for anyone wanting to implement Genius Hour with their learners. Packed with illustrations and templates it will also be a valuable resource for those who have already embarked on the Genius Hour journey.

– **Carolyn Stuart.** *Founder Weaving Futures Ltd*

"What a useful, easy to read and practical book from Karen Boyes. Teachers and students will benefit from this book with some excellent Project Based Learning ideas for the classroom and home. This book skilfully addresses 21st Century skills and gives teachers many great strategies to use in class. I wholeheartedly endorse it and congratulate Karen for addressing contemporary pedagogy in such a readable and enjoyable way. Genius Hour is pure genius!"

– **Dr Ian Lillico.** *Executive Director BoysForward Institute*

Published by Spectrum Education Limited,
P O Box 30 818, Lower Hutt, New Zealand

ISBN 978-0-9876647-7-8 (Paperback)
ISBN 978-0-9876647-8-5 (Kindle)

Text copyright © Karen Tui Boyes 2019

Designed and typeset by Spectrum Education, New Zealand

All rights reserved. No part of this publication may be reproduced, stored in a retrieval system, or transmitted in any form or by any means (electronic, mechanical, photocopying or otherwise), without the prior written permission of both the copyright owner and the publisher of this book.

Photos on pages 56, 57, 134-136 kindly supplied and printed with permission by Miriam Bell

Photos on pages 117, 122, 125 kindly supplied and printed with permission by Simon Ashby

Photos on pages 40-42, 95, 147-156 kindly supplied and printed with permission by Rachel O'Connell

Photos on pages 164-165 kindly supplied and printed with permission by Nik Edwards

This book is dedicated to Teachers with a passion for making students education meaningful and stimulating through real world learning that makes a positive impact on the world.

About The Author

Karen Tui Boyes is a champion for Life Long Learning across nations, industries and organisations. She is an author of *Creating An Effective Learning Environment*, and *Study Smart* and the creator of the Teachers Matter Magazine, Teachers Matter Conferences, Study Smart Boardgame, Study Smart Workshops and the Habits of Mind Bootcamp.

Karen is the CEO of Spectrum Education, Affiliate Director of the Institute for the Habits of Mind, and was awarded NZ Educator of the Year in 2014 & 2017, NZ Speaker of the Year in 2013 & 2019, and NZ Business Woman of the Year in 2001.

A sought after speaker who continually gets rave reviews from audiences around the world, Karen has presented across six continents, in 20 countries, and turns the latest educational research into easy-to-implement strategies and techniques.

She is wife of one and mother of two.

Tell me and I
FORGET

Teach me and I
REMEMBER

Involve me and I
LEARN

– BENJAMIN FRANKLIN

Contents

About The Author ix
Introduction 1

Part One
Chapter 1: Benefits of Genius Hour 9
Chapter 2: The Process of Genius Hour 13
Chapter 3: The Mechanics of How 69
Chapter 4: Assessment 77
Chapter 5: Common Challenges 81
Chapter 6: Struggling Students 85
Chapter 7: Explaining to Parents 89
Chapter 8: Underlying Assumptions 97
Chapter 9: Final Thoughts 111

Part Two: Practical Ideas from the Classroom
Chapter 10: A Game Changer: Simon Ashby 115
Chapter 11: A Rite of Passage: Miriam Bell 131
Chapter 12: A Bigger Impact: Rachel O'Connell 145
Chapter 13: A Whole Class Project: Nik Edwards 159
Chapter 14: Beyond The Basics: Kyle Hattie 167

Appendix 1: More Driving Questions Examples 187
Bibliography 191
Professional Development Options with Karen Tui Boyes 194
Stay in Touch with Karen 196
Gratitude & Thanks 197

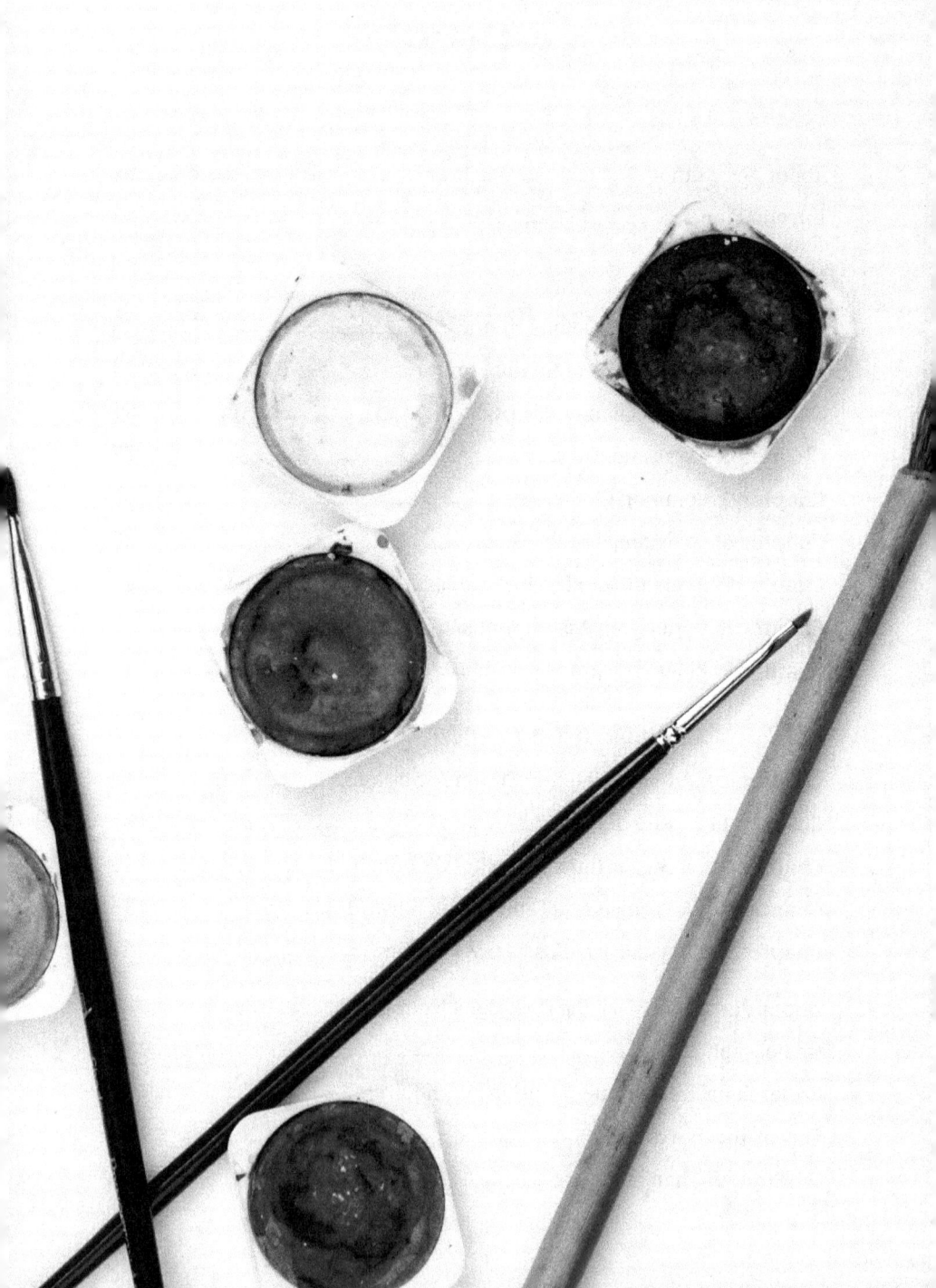

Introduction

Project based learning is becoming more popular in schools all over the world. It is seen as a way to engage learners, make learning more meaningful and give students the opportunity to explore something they are passionate about. It also gives students a sense that they can have an impact and make a difference in the world, whether locally, nationally or indeed globally.

Essentially, project based learning is a student centred pedagogy which involves an extended period of time for students to acquire a deeper knowledge through an active exploration of real world problems and challenges. It allows students freedom of expression, whilst recognising strengths, wonderings, passion and individual learning needs.

Genius Hour is a defined structure which allows students to explore something they are specifically passionate about.

A.J. Juliani, is a former middle school and high school English teacher and author of *Inquiry & Innovation in the Classroom: Using Genius Hour, 20% Time, and PBL to Drive Student Success*, describes Genius Hour as this:

❝ Genius Hour is a movement that allows students to explore their own passions and encourages creativity in the classroom. It provides students a choice in what they learn during a set period of time during school. ❞

The idea for Genius Hour possibility originates from the company Google. During 2004, in an attempt to empower employees to be more creative and innovative, founders Larry Page and Sergey Brin announced a new philosophy called Twenty Percent Time. They encouraged employees, alongside their other projects, to spend 20% of their time working on what they thought might benefit the company the most.

Many of their new products came from this initiative, including Gmail, Google maps, Google News, Adsense and Google Talk.

Whilst this Google programme looks very different today, other companies also followed their lead with LinkedIn running an InCubator programme giving engineers time away from their day-to-day work in order to develop their own product ideas; Apple has Blue Sky which allows some employees to spend a few weeks on projects of their choice and Microsoft has a programme called The Garage which allows employees to experiment and build their own projects using Microsoft resources.

Part of the appeal behind these initiatives was employee satisfaction which lead to better retention. In his 2009 book, *Drive – The Surprising Truth About What Motivates Us*, Daniel Pink states; "This type of intrinsic motivation highly outweighs any type of external motivation."

These ideas of wanting students to be intrinsically motivated and providing time for students to focus on what they are passionate about has led to a 'movement', as AJ Juliani sees it, called Genius Hour.

Genius Hour is a great way to teach and reinforce 21st Century Skills, life skills and showcase problem solving strategies in a real world way. It is guaranteed there will be frustration, learnings about time management, prioritising, problems to solve – which keeps it real and maximises learning opportunities.

So… what if students could learn about anything they wanted? What if teachers and schools put the students at the centre of the curriculum for a segment of the learning week?

This book explores the process of how to introduce, facilitate and celebrate the process of Genius Hour. The first half delves into the seven stages of Genius Hour whilst the second section gives insights into five teachers' classrooms and how they have used the process in a practical manner. They have outlined their processes, adaptations, challenges and wins. This will allow you to see, how with experience, this process grows, changes and adapts to the students in your classroom and the bigger purpose of the curriculum.

The ideas in this book come from a vast many teachers I have had the pleasure of working alongside and observing on my travels around the world. I have assisted many schools to implement Genius Hour into their classrooms and coached teachers through this process.

I am indebted to all those teachers who have shared with me their insights, challenges and great successes through this wonderful process of Genius Hour.

You will also find the black line masters are available for download at

www.spectrumeducation.com/project-genius-book-resources

These have been designed and adapted from my own work and that of the teachers I have had a pleasure of working alongside.

Personally, I prefer not to give students the blackline master templates to fill out, when requiring thinking – as this can restrict students thinking to only filling in the template. My preference is to teach students how to use a thinking process by modelling it with the class and giving students blank paper to design their own. This allows for flexibility and creativity. I am providing the blackline masters for your reference and to use how you see most appropriate.

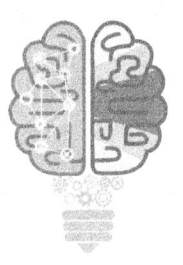

Part One

CHAPTER ONE

The Benefits of Genius Hour

Genius Hour encourages a focus on students solving real world problems or challenges provided by the teacher. It is inter-disciplinary as these problems are not solved using only one curriculum area, since they use skills and knowledge across multiple subject areas. It creates meaningful opportunities for learning and connection between syllabus areas rather than students learning subjects in isolation. Genius Hour is a holistic process with students involved in inquiry, problem solving and product construction. This is a learning by doing process.

Students, for example, may be learning how to write a persuasive speech during the pitch stage and then speech and delivery techniques at the final Presentation stage. Blogging, diarying and recording progress may also tick some of the literacy outcomes. Whilst doing this, students may also be creating videos, podcasts and audio files from the design and technology curriculum. Alongside this art, numeracy, history and social sciences may be covered.

Genius Hour provides an element of rigour not seen in many curriculum areas as it calls for the application of knowledge and skills and not just recognition and recall. It is far more complex than simple rote learning as students are required to apply their knowledge and skills in different contexts which often go beyond curriculum areas.

Another element of this process means students are learning and presenting for a wider audience, not just for the teachers or examiner as happens in traditional education. This means they are involved in the learning and are using the four C's of 21st Century Learning: Critical Thinking, Collaboration, Communication and Creativity.

With a strong student centred approach Genius Hour not only helps to cultivate the four C's it also provides students opportunities to foster ownership, decision making skills, team work, communication skills, time and resource management, accountability and so on. These are all important not only in school, but in tertiary study and beyond school in the work place and the home.

Students are usually encouraged to work individually to sharpen their ability to develop self-discipline and self-directed life and work skills. Teachers report higher academic achievement and an increased motivation to learn when students develop these self-management skills.

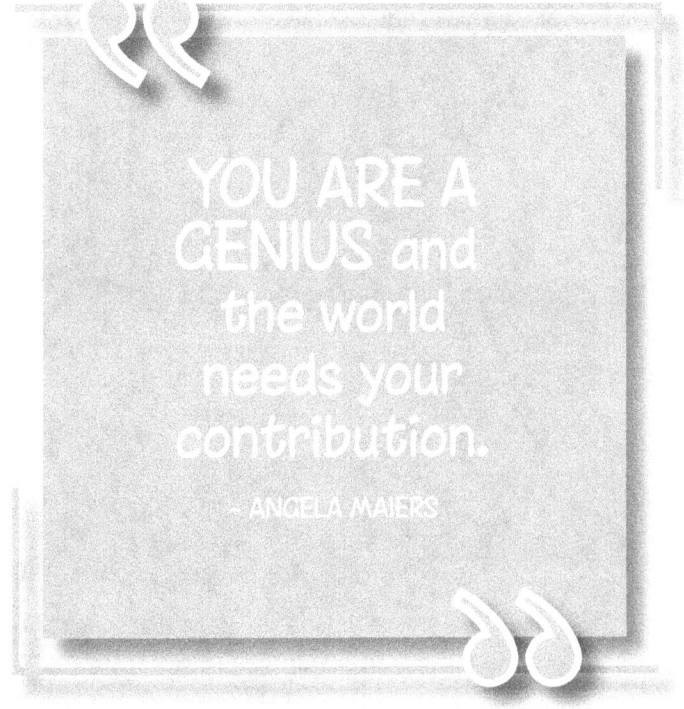

CHAPTER TWO

The Process of Genius Hour

Project based learning though Genius Hour provides a structure to help students succeed.

There are three main components to Genius Hour.

1. **Research:** Students must research something. Students cannot spend time going over information they already know. The key is learning and as a bi-product of this, learning and refining research skills.

2. **Create:** Students have to create something. They need to have something 'to show' for their time.

3. **Present:** Students have to present something. At the end of the time frame given, students give a verbal presentation to explain their process and learning.

When starting out using Genius Hour in your classroom, it is useful to stick closely to the process outlined. Once you become more confident you can and most certainly will modify and adapt the process to suit both your students and the learning outcomes.

Introducing Genius Hour

A great place to start is with a discussion about what it means to be a genius. If students are going to spend time each week being 'geniuses' defining what this means and how it will apply to them is essential.

Chat about what are some of the attributes of a genius. Not only are they smart, they are also insightful, creative, persistent and continuous learners. What other attributes might your students add? Brainstorm a list of attributes and actions that students consider to be ingenious.

You might also have students research or simply share with them the origins of Genius Hour.

Advertise the fact that students will be engaging in an exciting Genius Hour time with posters and teasers. I saw a huge poster in a classroom saying, "Genius Hour is Approaching" and another that said, "Genius Hour – what impact do you want to make?"

The Seven Steps

Genius Hour is based on a process of seven steps. These steps provide a clear structure and pathway from beginning to end.

1. Find your Passion
2. Plan, Plan, Plan
3. Make a Pitch
4. Project
5. Create a Product
6. Presentation Day
7. Ponder

Let's look at each step in more depth...

Step 1: Find Your Passion

Start by discussing, "What does it mean to be passionate about something?" This links with the concept of joy and happiness. Invite students to brainstorm things they are passionate about. What do they love doing for fun?

Create a wonder wall and invite students to add questions they have about the world. What are they curious about? What do they wonder about? This may serve as an idea generator or simply spark inspiration.

Show students videos such as Cain's Arcade or the Kid President's Pep Talk, both easily found on YouTube. I particularly enjoy the Kid President as he talks about some key aspects which link directly with Genius Hour.

Great quotes from the Kid President include…

- "The world needs you to stop being boring. Boring is easy. Everyone can be boring. But you are gooder than that!"
- "We can make every day better for each other"
- "You were made to be awesome!"

- "It's everyone's job to give the world a reason to thank us"

- "Create something that will make the world awesome"

For some students this step can be a challenge as they are not used to being able to choose in the school environment. For others it is the most natural and easiest step to take.

Tournament Planning

A great way to get students thinking is by using a Tournament Plan. On one edge of the paper have students list all the things they love doing, are curious about or have always wanted to create, make or do. On the opposite edge, create a list of what bothers, annoys them or they dislike in the world. Now start at one edge and compare the first two ideas – and then ask; "Which of the two would win a contest for your favourite?" Continue down the list doing this with all the pairs. Complete the same process on the other side of the page, except this time which of the two ideas concerns them most?

Continue this process comparing two ideas until they end up with one idea from each side.

This process can be either very enlightening or take major creatively to see how the two ideas might relate.

The photo below is of a student's tournament plan. She ended up with a 'like' of drawing and 'dislike' of her Cousin having cancer! Pondering on this for a while she decided her passion project would be a series of videos to teach her cousin how to draw which might improve her relationship with him, as well as give him a focus while in treatment.

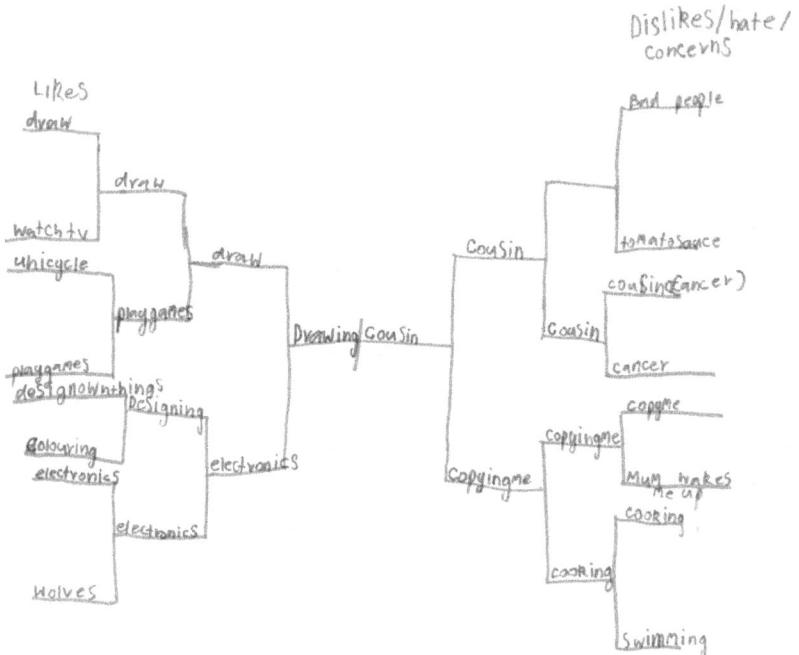

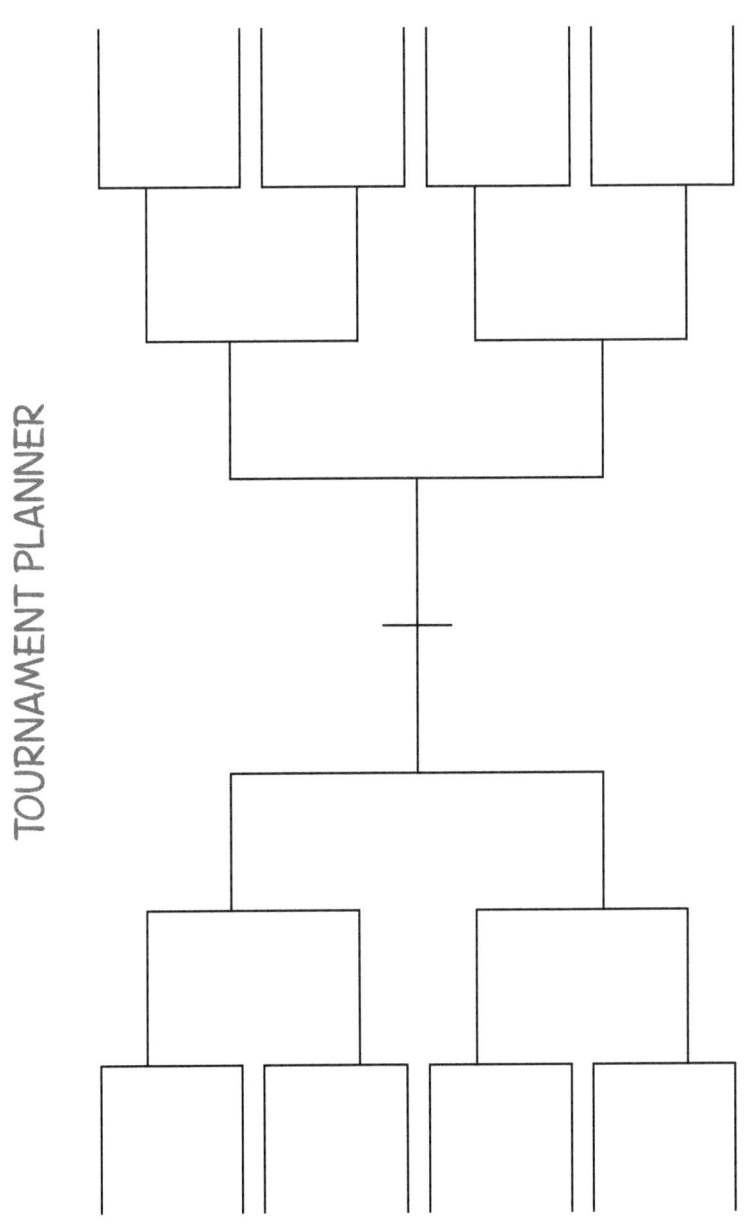

Bad Idea Brainstorm

If you are working with older students, teacher, author and speaker Kevin Brookhouser uses a Bad Idea Brainstorm to help generate ideas. He has students brainstorm all the ideas that would be a bad idea for Genius Hour. Whilst this creates hilarity – it also highlights some ideas that with creativity and finessing could be great project topics.

Questioning

Question students as to what they like doing when no-one is telling them what to do. Sample questions include;

- What do you love doing in the weekend?
- What do you enjoy doing in the school holidays?
- What would you do if you could do anything?
- What have you considered making or creating?
- What do you love reading or watching? Is there a topic or theme?
- If you won Lotto, what would you do with your time?
- In whose life would you like to make a difference?

Many times, the answers to these questions will be activities that consume time such as watching tv, playing online games, social media, watching YouTube videos etc. or they may be activities which are about the communication of time. These include hanging out with friends, talking with friends, chatting online, etc. Ask students if they ever consider creating or making something during these times. Maybe it is a problem of frustration they would like to solve.

Have students hone in on what type of information do they like to read or watch. Maybe it is sports, fantasy, fashion related or history, etc. The more specific they can be the easier it will be to identify a passion or focus.

If they are not sure, invite them to choose their favourite four ideas and spend a few days exploring or creating with that passion. It may just help clarify their passion.

Talk to students about the 'state of flow.' This is a positive psychology term also known as being in the 'zone.' Wikipedia defines it as, "A mental state of operation in which a person performing an activity is fully immersed in a feeling of energised focus, full involvement and enjoyment of the activity."

Other focusing questions include;

- What are five things you wish you physically could do?
- What are five hobbies you have always wanted to try
- What do you never have time for and would love to do?
- What is something you wish you could always make?
- Name something that does not exist, and might benefit your school, community or world.

This is perhaps one of the hardest parts of the Genius Hour process. Sometimes students really struggle with coming up with a project idea and question. As a teacher, use your best judgment. Maybe invite them to google search what other students have done. You might steer them towards a project with the school caretaker, or an expert you know who will be able to keep them engaged. Partnering up with a friend might be a possibility as well.

You will find some great project ideas in the latter chapters of this book. There is also a list at the end of the book.

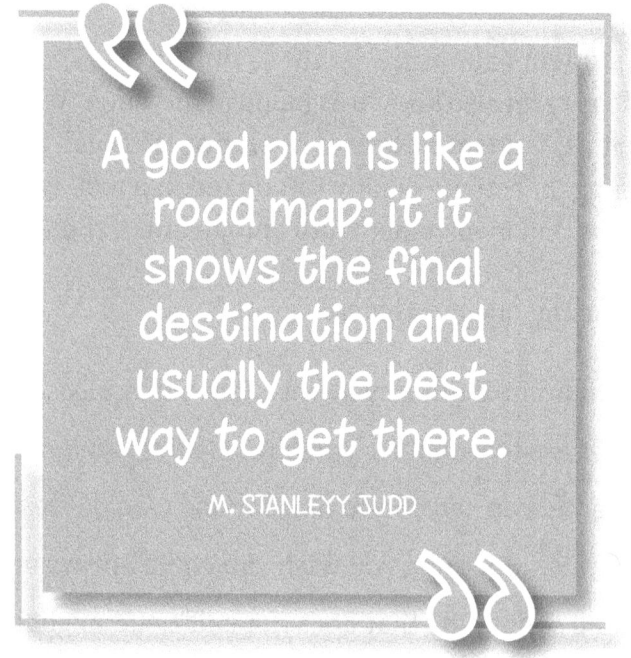

A good plan is like a road map: it it shows the final destination and usually the best way to get there.

M. STANLEYY JUDD

Step 2: Plan, Plan, Plan

Time management guru, Alan Lakein is well known for saying *"Failing to plan is planning to fail,"* and speaker Dale Carnegie said, *"An hour of planning can save you ten hours of doing."*

Encourage and provide time for students to plan out their project. This is one of the most important steps for success in Genius Hour.

Stephen Covey, educator and author, advocated for 'starting with the end in mind.' Have students become clear on their end goal and plan backward from there. If that is where they want to end up in x number of weeks, what will they need to achieve along the way? Ultimately at this step, students will create a step by step plan to know exactly what they need to do each week in Genius Hour time.

Of course, this part, for many students is a piece of the ultimate learning, such as planning too much or too little, knowing your own limitations and strengths or being able to predict potential problems or challenges. Be mindful to allow students to have some of these learnings.

Create a Driving Question

Just as great scientists and explorers start with a question., it is important for each Genius Hour project to have a driving or guiding question. This needs to be something that is not Googleable, yet can be researched.

To make questions non Googleable, a question may require reframing. For example, instead of asking, "How high can a hot air balloon fly?" ask, "What makes a hot air balloon fly?" Change the question 'How fast can a cat run?' to "what makes a cat run so fast?"

Spend time on getting the question and project clear as this will alleviate some of the challenges later.

Guiding questions might start with;

- Am I able to…?
- Can I learn more about…?
- What makes a great…?
- Can we find out why…?
- How can we…?
- How do I plan…?
- What causes…?
- How can I teach…?

Typically, the question will have many different answers or solutions and may never be fully answered.

Driving Questions Examples from Clutha Valley School

- How might I design a water filter for a lower cost?
- How can we create wearable arts on a budget?
- How might I develop an understanding of how music is composed and create my own music using readily available resources?
- How can we use old jewellery to make new jewellery?
- How might we design a self-propelled car that can travel 25 metres or more?
- How can we create music with recycled materials?
- How could I bake on a budget but it still tastes good?
- How might I make a new sport that everyone will enjoy?
- How might we design and make a rocket that will reach over 100m?

Other students have asked...

- How can we inform people about tidal erosion in our community?
- Can I design an engaging board game to help students learn their basic facts?
- Can I make a healthy sweet?
- Why are women often portrayed as the weaker sex in movies?
- How might I teach others to play netball?
- How can I stop people smoking?
- In what ways can we make exercise fun?
- Can I redesign the school playground to be more fun?

There are more examples at the end of the book.

This process requires modelling by the teacher and for students to be coached through designing a suitable question. You might brainstorm ideas and examples from the wondering's students have and put them in a question form. I particularly enjoy using the 'Fishbowl' protocol for this.

Fishbowl Protocol

Ask for a volunteer to have their topic and driving question coached by you in front of the class. Choose someone who is not quite sure if they have a clear question. This student is then in the 'fishbowl' while everyone else initially watches the process from the outside.

Invite the student to explain their passion and proposed topic. Ask questions to clarify their thought process, deepen their thinking and craft the question.

It might sound like this...

> T: "Please explain your topic and ideas you have been thinking about for your project."
>
> S: "Well, I really love cricket and wanted to do something about that."
>
> T: "Great. What is it you love about cricket?"
>
> S: "I really like bowling and umpiring."
>
> T: "If you had to choose between the two which might you choose?"
>
> S: "Hmmm, probably umpiring as I like being out on the field."
>
> T: "As you think about umpiring, what part of it would you like to investigate?"
>
> S: "I've been thinking about learning how to umpire the games for school."
>
> T: "What do you know about umpiring already?"

S: "I know the rules."

T: "Which part of umpiring do you find challenging?"

S: "Mostly my ability to concentrate for a long time – sometimes I zone out a bit."

T: "So might that be an area you could research?"

S: "Yes."

T: "What might your question be?"

S: "What are some of the tips and techniques umpires use to concentrate when out on the field?"

T: turns to the students watching… "Is that an ungoogleable question? One that will stretch this S to learn?"

The teacher may coach the student further to look at how this project might have a bigger impact on others. The student may decide to make an infographic that can be shared with local or national cricket club, or create a YouTube channel for umpires to share their tips. It could be a short video with tips shared. The possibilities are abundant. You may ask the students watching to add ideas at this stage.

Once the students have watched you coach a couple more students, invite students to work in pairs to coach each other.

Kyle Hattie (contributing author in chapter 14) gives this example:

Year 4 Student: "We are wanting to feed the homeless for Christmas time."

Teacher: "That sounds like a great project. How are you going to do that?"

Year 4 Student: "We will walk around town giving them sandwiches. There are a lot of homeless people there."

Teacher: "Well let's think about how we can do something with our community so that we are reaching more."

Year 4 Student: Pauses to rethink her idea. Year 5 student who is working with her, "My last school donated canned food. We can do that."

Teacher "Great thinking. Let's plan it out." And that is how it started—two students who just wanted to help out others for their passion project. Neither student thought that their little project could turn into a community initiative that would get them into the local newspaper. But that is exactly what happened.

This fishbowl protocol may be used in many areas of the Genius Hour Projects and curriculum areas in your classroom.

Students feed homeless this Christmas

Ormiston Primary School students have a plan to help the homeless this Christmas. If the efforts of three Ormiston Primary School students are anything to go by, the homeless in Manukau will be receiving more than just loose change for Christmas this year.

Students Seraya Wells (eight), Kim Lim (nine) and Annia Ramirez (10) have started a food can drive for the homeless, with the goal of collecting 500 cans by Christmas.

They've decorated the school with posters, told their friends what's happening, and are eagerly awaiting the arrival of cans from their peers, to be distributed by Salvation Army at the end of the project.

"We're up to the part where we're starting to collect cans," says Ms Lim, "and there will definitely be a prize for whoever has the most – we're just not sure what that is yet!"

Ms Wells says one of her favourite things about Christmas is the opportunity to help people and give a gift to somebody in need – something all three of the girls are putting into action this festive season.

Learning coach Kyle Hattie says he is proud of the girls for their initiative, and hopes to see more projects like this come out of the school's iExplore programme.

iExplore is one of three learning blocks at Ormiston Primary School, giving students designated time to create, plan and implement a project of their choice.

Mr Hattie says the girls aren't the only ones who have successfully put their project into practice.

Eight-year-old Ronav Naicker wanted a place to ride his bike, so he used his time in iExplore to design a bike track for the school.

The year three student was given approval to implement his project after making a presentation to the school's Board of Trustees, and has contracted the Bike On New Zealand Charitable Trust to make the project a reality as part of its national Bikes in Schools programme.

Mr Hattie says there is currently no timeframe on the project, but confirmed the school has given it the go-ahead and will see it through.

Ormiston Primary School students (from left) Kim Lim, Annia Ramirez and Seraya Wells aim to raise 500 cans for the homeless this Christmas.

Planning the Project

Once a driving question has been found, invite students to think through the process and plan out their next steps. Obviously, students don't know what they don't know, and this step may require more teacher guidance and for many students the 'not knowing' will be part of their significant learning.

Ask students to consider the following…

- What do I need to find out?

- What are the action steps they will take?
- Create a timeline of these actions
- What resources may be required?
- Who might act as a mentor or helper?
- How are you going to share your project?
- What barriers might I come up against?
- What is the end goal?

Know The Why

As Kyle Hattie explains in chapter 14, ensuring students know why and what they are learning is important. Having a purpose or a bigger reason than themselves can also add to the motivation. As Miriam Bell (see more in chapter 11) explained: learning to crochet is a skill, however crocheting scarves for orphans gives a higher motivation to keep going when it gets hard or tedious.

Individual or team projects?

Students may choose to work together or individually, or you as the teacher may decide. Working with others requires co-operation, team work and great communication skills to ensure the equal division of labour. This is best worked through in this planning stage.

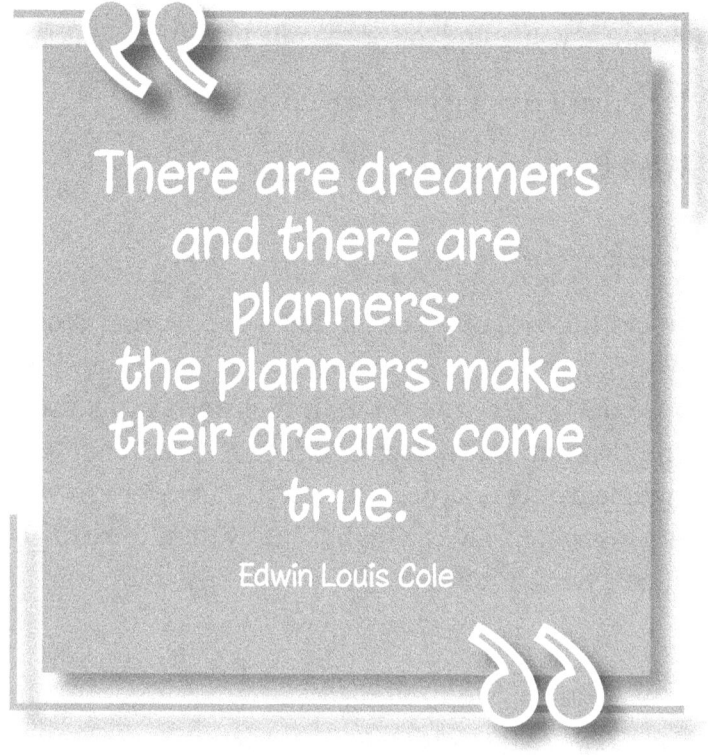

> There are dreamers and there are planners; the planners make their dreams come true.
>
> Edwin Louis Cole

Planning

Record 1-3 guiding questions for this project	
Describe why this is important to you, and/or the world. (What is your motivation?)	
Outline some of the first steps you will take to get your project started.	
What do you intend to create?	
List the materials and resources you will require.	
Who do you need to contact to find out more information or who might you need to help you with this project? How would you contact them? (email, phone, in person, skype etc)	
Create a draft timeline and milestones to achieve this project and your goals.	
In what ways are you planning to present the knowledge you have learned during this project?	
List some of the potential barriers you predict may occur during this project and what might you do to minimise these?	
What impact would you like your project to make? Who would you like to impact?	

Project Genius

Step 3: Making a Pitch

The purpose of making a pitch is for students to get further clarity, feedback and to gain approval for their project. There are a couple of ways this step is typically conducted.

The pitch could be a short verbal presentation which helps the student to clarify their project as well as gain valuable feedback from their peers or it may be a proposal submitted to the teacher for approval. It could even be a combination of both.

This stage can either happen before or after the planning stage - depending on how you wish to structure this in your classroom.

Guidelines for this stage include:

- Having at least 1-3 clear inquiry based questions
- Your motivation for this topic (justify why you should be spending your time on this)
- What you intend to create
- Materials possibly required

- Expert help that may be sought
- Timeline of milestones to reach the goal
- How you might present your project

If students are giving a verbal pitch I use a 1-2 minute time frame (maximum) and ask them to address these areas...

- Describe your motivation for why you are wanting to do this project
- Outline your timeline, resources and goals
- Explain your proposed product you will be creating to share at the end

This part may be linked into your literacy programme and I prefer students to deliver this pitch as a persuasive speech. I want them to convince me that what they want to do is a good idea, worthy of their classroom time. I liken it to a commercial – you want your students to 'sell' their idea in a creative and interesting way.

I use a 1-2 minute time frame and keep this tight. The purpose of this is to encourage concise clarity.

Ask a student to be a time keeper and give a warning when they have 10-20 seconds to go. At 1-2 minutes or close after, at the end of a sentence – or when the student pauses to breathe – either ask the audience to applaud or play some loud, positive music – just like they do at the Academy Awards!

Obviously, I am not advocating throwing students into the deep end with the pitch by being unprepared. Give students an opportunity to practise their pitch with a small group. I use this protocol process.

Pitch Practice Protocol

1. Team students in groups of 4 and ask them to share their Genius Hour project topics with each other.

2. Give each person 3-5 minutes to share and receive feedback from their team mates. (Time this and let them know when it is time to change to the next person.)

3. Provide time for students to use the feedback and draft their 1-2 minute pitch. It is worth noting that professional speakers plan for around 80% of the time allocated as there is usually adlibbing during the actual presentation. Furthermore, an average adult speaks at about 250 words per minute – so a 2 minute talk will have approximately 500 words. This will differ depending on the age of your students. You may only allow 1 minute for the pitch – it is up to you, your time frame and which skills you would like your students to learn.

4. In their group of four, one student gives their pitch. It is useful for a listener to time the 1-2 minutes, so they get a sense of how long it is. Once the talk is given,

invite the group to give feedback and do it again. (You may also facilitate the whole class through this with you as the timer – giving 2 minutes for the pitch, 60 seconds for feedback etc.)

5. Each person should give their pitch three times before the next person has a turn. This will take approximately 40 minutes (or 20 minutes if you do this in pairs) and can be conducted during a literacy session or part of your Genius Hour time. It is OK for students to have their notes for this session and feedback can be on the content of the presentation and/or their presentation skills. This again may depend on the depth of learning, integration of other core subjects and your time frame.

6. The next day, or next Genius Hour, run the actual pitch session. Students may use cue cards, their notes or talk from their memory. Encourage students not to read their notes as it is a pitch not a public reading session.

7. After each student has given their pitch, I give the audience (the rest of the class) a moment to reflect on what they heard and to use a Gems and Opportunities feedback process.

> Feedback is the breakfast of champions.
> Ken Blanchard

Gems & Opportunities Feedback Protocol

This a great way to invite students to give and receive feedback given to me by one of my colleagues and friends, Dr Rich Allen. After a student has given their presentation, they then ask for feedback from their peers. The student chooses who gives the feedback firstly receiving 2-3 gems (what they did well) and then 2-3 opportunities (ways to improve or questions the person may want to consider). During this process, the student receiving the feedback is allowed to say only two words "Thank you." This stops any justification, excuses and the need for them to have to add to their presentation.

It is wise to pause between the end of the presentation and the feedback giving, to allow the audience time to think about what they might say. Extra feedback can also be written on post-it notes and given to the student later.

Empowering the student to choose who gives the feedback keeps them in control of the process and receptive to the responses. After you have facilitated this process a few times, encourage students to choose people who are not in their close circle of friends to give feedback.

The pitch may also be given as a Power Point presentation, a Powtow, a mini movie – however much of this takes further scaffolding and time. It will depend on your bigger goals for your students and class, their prior knowledge and your time frame.

Personally, I see that Power Points are often used only as a tool for the students to read from, rather than an aid to enhance the learning and understanding. Furthermore, in 1-2 minutes there is little time for students to watch and listen at the same time. The impact of the message is often lost.

Make this session fun and exciting ☺

Rachel O'Connell (see more from Rachel in chapter 12) adds a fun step here. Once projects are approved, students create a google drawing which is then displayed in the classroom to spark interest and conversations.

Following are examples of these posters from Rachel's classroom.

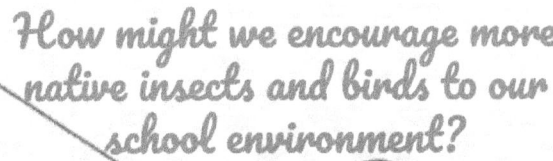

Chapter 2: The Process of Genius Hour

Project Genius

Chapter 2: The Process of Genius Hour

Pitch Presentation

What is your motivation for doing this project?
What impact do you want to make?

Outline your timeline, resources and goals.

Explain your end product and how this will help you make your desired impact.

"Just Do It!
- NIKE"

Step 4: The Project

This is where students get on with it! Students will be researching, working with experts, creating prototypes, creating and putting their action plan into place.

Students may be accessing information online, through apps, books, magazines, surveys, phoning or skyping experts etc.

This is when your classroom will get extra busy. With so many different and varied projects going on, having a set of rules may be useful.

Here are some I recommend:

Rules for Genius Hour

1. *You must work the entire time. Genius Hour is a time to focus and get into action.*

2. *If you need materials, you must bring them from home.* As a teacher you cannot be responsible for 20-30 different projects and their resources. This is an opportunity to foster and reinforce responsibility.

3. *If you have not completed your core work and must do's, you cannot participate in Genius Hour.*
   Stephen Covey calls this #firstthingsfirst. Genius Hour is far more than inquiry and project based learning. It is an opportunity for students to learn about priorities in life. The 'Eat your veggies before you get any pudding,' philosophy.

4. *If you have to be warned twice, your Genius Hour is over for today.*
   Behavioural expectations need to be high and having consequences is important. This is not a time for mucking around or being unfocused.

5. *Your project is due on the day, regardless of how many Genius Hour you miss.*
   Again, a big life lesson lurks here. A deadline is a deadline and extension of deadlines often leads to others feeling it is unfair or unjust. In life, if I am late paying my taxes, there are penalties. It does not matter if I have been away on holiday, it was my child's birthday or if I was so busy I forgot, there will be a fine. The same applies in life with time agreements. If the Interview is at 4pm and you turn up at 4.15pm (without any notification of the lateness – yes things happen such as a flat tyre) then the employer can assume you are not reliable.

6. *Clean up all your materials at the end of the Genius Hour.*
   The last thing you need as a teacher is to have to clean

up after all your students. Again, this is about responsibility and organisation.

Research

There are many ways students can go about researching for their project. These include:

- Internet using reliable sources
- Books on the subject – non fiction
- Encyclopedia
- Dictionary
- Magazines
- Newspapers
- Talking to parents, teachers and others with an interest in the topic
- Interview with someone who has knowledge or expertise of the topic.

If you are concerned about students accessing random websites, you may wish to create cards with QR codes of sites you recommend.

You can simply generate QR codes at *www.qr-code-generator.com* or scan the image on the right which will take you to this site.

Tips for summarising

Summarising

1. Highlight the main ideas in the text you want to summarise (do not include any minor details)

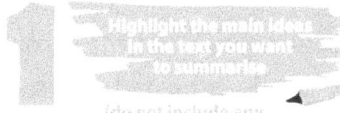

2. Combine these ideas together in your own words

3. Correctly interpret the original

4. Do not include your own opinion or add extra information

opinion ≠ fact

5. Use your own words and not those of the original author (unless using quotation marks)

6. Remember to cite your source using a recognised referencing format

7. Keep reminding your reader that you are summarising the work of someone else by using the following phrases:

"The author goes on to say that ..."
"The text further states that ..."

www.spectrumeducation.com

Even if students have kid-friendly websites to use, it is still worth monitoring as many of the sites contain adverts.

Encourage students to keep a bibliography of their sources and to check for the credibility of the information from all sources.

If your students are new to researching – it pays to take the time to conduct a mini lesson on note-taking and documenting resources.

As students work, you can conduct short 1-1 meetings to check on their progress, answer questions and check their general understanding of the information they are researching and discovering.

My Bibliography

Books:
Author (last name first) _____
Title: _____
Publication date: _____ Publisher: _____

Author (last name first) _____
Title: _____
Publication date: _____ Publisher: _____

Websites:
Author: (last name first) _____
Title of Article (if any) _____
Publication date: _____ Website: _____
URL: _____

Author: (last name first) _____
Title of Article (if any) _____
Publication date: _____ Website: _____
URL: _____

Author: (last name first) _____
Title of Article (if any) _____
Publication date: _____ Website: _____
URL: _____

Magazine/Newspaper
Author: (last name first) _____
Title of Article: _____
Title of Magazine/Newspaper: _____
Publication. Date: _____ Pages: _____

Record the Journey

Another key to success is to have students record the journey as they go. It is too late in the last week before the big reveal to have to think about the learning, frustrations, failures, challenges and successes along the way. Encourage students to spend time each week blogging or journaling their progress.

You may provide a template for students to do this on or provide guidelines. It may be in a blog, on a shared Google doc or a Power Point to be shared or edited later.

This also may be combined with your literacy time.

A great idea is to stop 5-10 minutes before the end of their first project session and model how to fill out their reflection form. They may fill these out at the end of a session, for homework or in a literacy session.

At the end of each session it is also useful to ask a couple of students to share 'where they are at.' This will help give the class a sense of momentum and progress, plus an insight into how other projects are going.

Progress Report For _____ Week # _____

What was your goal for Genius Hour this week with your project?	
What did you accomplish with your project this week? (be specific)	
What is your goal for next week?	
What are some of the key things you learnt this week about your topic?	
What did you learn about yourself this week?	
Did you make any changes to your project idea this week? If so, what were they?	
What materials or resources might you need next week?	
What problems or challenges did you face this week? What did you do to overcome them? How might you fix them?	
Did you add to your bibliography this week?	
What are some of your goals for next week?	

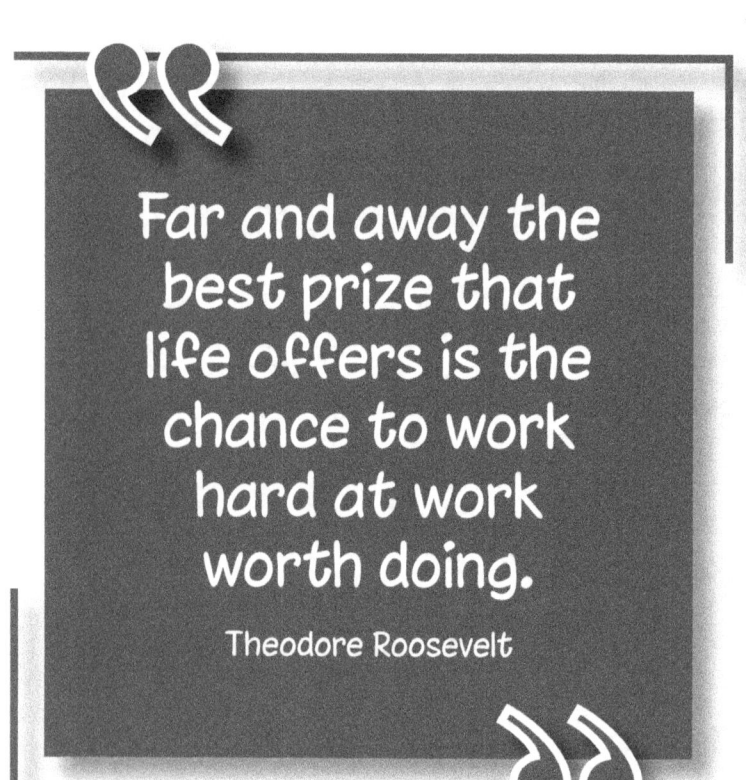

> Far and away the best prize that life offers is the chance to work hard at work worth doing.
>
> Theodore Roosevelt

Step 5: The Product

This is the step where students show the bigger application of their project. The impact and difference they have made to themselves, others, the environment or the planet.

Questions at this stage include: What did you create? What can you show to demonstrate your learning? Does your product match up with your initial planning and goal?

It needs to show the effort, thinking, time and consideration of others.

The product is designed to be shared with the others. The final product may, and I believe should be shared to the world via YouTube, some form of prototype, a digital book, website or recorded demonstration etc.

Examples of products from Miriam Bell's Classroom are shown on the following pages.

Jack acted on the results of an earlier survey our class undertook as a part of a statistics unit regarding the state of our local community swimming pool. Using 'SketchUp', he updated the changing / toilet facilities to meet current

regulations and user suggestions, and redesigned the landscaping, utilising native plants and retaining. He then made a scale model from custom wood,
priced the project, and has submitted his design and costings to the local pool committee.

Will used 'SketchUp' to design a new local sports facility that could house the many sporting clubs in the Waimakariri area. He then built a scale model and priced his design, including land purchase.

Ethan showing the development of his copper rose design, from first attempt, through to Mark V. These are being sold through a local boutique store,
and are made almost entirely from offcuts and scrap.

Jake and Liam worked on making a gun cabinet, made according to legal requirements. Materials and tools were provided by a local builder.

Hannah learned to crochet, and sent scarves over to a Romanian orphanage.

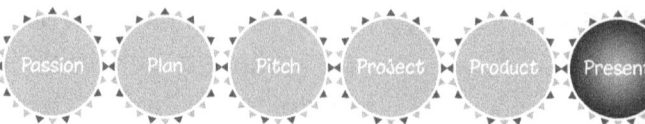

Step 6: The Presentation

The opportunity to share the product with an authentic audience is a huge key to the success of Genius Hour. It shows students that learning and the impact they can have is beyond the walls of a classroom, school gates, the community, town or even country borders! It makes the learning more relevant, meaningful and gives it far more purpose.

This is the stage where all the learning and hard work comes together. It is an opportunity to present and share wins, failures, learnings and challenges with a short talk.

A quick search in Pinterest or Google and you will find a wonderful graphic of 101 Ways to Show You Know. Allowing students to show their learning in many different ways provides wonderful differentiation to the classroom.

This may include:

- Visuals such as a poster, diorama, timeline, map etc.
- Written, such as a book, newspaper article, glossary, questionnaire, etc

- Performance, such as a dance, a play, video, music performance and so on

- Spoken, such as a rap, script, rhyme, lesson, news report ...

One rule I enforce is that if a student made a poster last time, they cannot make another. If they love doing stop motion animation, then I allow one per year. This simply helps students develop more skills and ways of showing knowledge. Each time they repeat the same method of presentation, I would also expect them to be improving their skill over time.

Create a sign-up sheet for presentation order. Students love being able to sign up before the due date.

Presentation Structure

Students new to giving presentations may initially require a structure to plan and work towards.

Here is a simple structure for Genius Hour Projects:

1. *Your Motivation:* Describe your motivation behind your Genius Hour project and what impact you wanted to make.

2. *Your Plan:* Briefly outline what you planned you could actually do, or you wanted to achieve.

3. *Your Challenges*: What were your learning struggles and challenges? Tell a funny or frustrating story to illustrate your journey.

4. *Your Product:* Quickly show, explain or demo (30 secs or less) what you have produced from your research. The audience will have a chance on Presentation Day to view these before your talk.

5. *Learning Wins:* What were your learning wins? What went well and what did you learn about yourself in the process?

6. *The Result:* Explain what you made and your reward for this and the impact you have made.

7. *Implications and Reflection*: What are your next steps? Where to from here? What would you like to do next time?

Depending on your student's capacity and prior experience, and even the number of students in your class along with the time factor, these presentations might be 3-5 minutes in duration.

Presentation Day

Invite family, friends, their experts and the community to this day. Make it a BIG deal as it is a celebration of the work and learning over the past weeks.

In the morning of the presentation day, invite students to set up their Genius Hour display showcasing their product, process and learnings.

Start the presentation time with a thanks to all those who have helped and supported the students.

Encourage the audience to spend time walking around the displays, asking questions of the students about their learnings, challenges and processes. Allow about 45 mins for this.

Next the students give their presentations. There is no feedback given, however encourage and expect wild applause from the audience, acknowledging the learning and the courage to give their talk.

Finally finish with a grand afternoon tea or an appropriate celebration for your students and community.

Presentation Practice

Ensure you give time and support for students to practice their talk. You may follow a similar process as with the pitch protocol, as outlined below.

Once the students have drafted their talk, in pairs invite them to practice at least three times, gaining feedback from their partner before swapping. For a three minute presentation plan for 2.5 minutes and for a 5 minute talk, plan for 4.5 minutes.

Your students may have a Power Point slide show, create a Pow Tow or show a video they have put together as part of their presentation. This does add more time and complexity to giving a presentation and will depend on your students' capacity and motivation.

Presentation Tips

A few success tips to impart to your students...

- Show your enthusiasm! – Remember this is a project you have a passion for. Let that excitement show!
- Speak loudly and clearly. Be confident in your words and your knowledge.

- Use your notes/cards. You are not expected to memorise your presentation - have your notes to keep you on track.

- Look at your audience. This is a talk, not a public reading. People will listen more if you look at them.

- Avoid reading from the screen, as you will have your back to the audience. Consider blanking the slides when you are not referring to them.

- Pause, smile and breathe throughout your talk.

- Finish off with a summarising conclusion, wondering or action you want to leave the audience with. Make sure your ending shows what you have learned.

- Take questions at the end. This is your chance to show your expertise and knowledge.

Record the Presentations

My preference is to record each presentation and share these widely. The bigger the audience the more people a student can inspire and impact. Ensure you have student and parental permission if the video is being shared publicly on the web. These videos can also be used as a self-evaluation tool.

The Presentation

1. *Your Motivation:* Describe your motivation behind your Genius Hour project and what impact you wanted to make.

2. *Your Plan:* Briefly outline what you planned you could actually do or you wanted to achieve.

3. *Your Challenges:* What were your learning struggles and challenges? Tell a funny or frustrating story to illustrate your journey.

4. *Your product:* Quickly show, explain or demo (30 secs or less) what you have produced from your research. The audience will have a chance on Presentation Day to view these before your talk.

5. *Learning Wins:* What were your learning wins? What went well and what did you learn about yourself in the process?

6. Explain what you made and your reward for this, and the impact you have made.

7. *Implications and Reflection:* What are your next steps? Where to from here? What would you like to do next time?

Download at www.spectrumeducation.com/project-genius-book-resources

Step 7: Ponder

After the event, provide time for students to ponder on their project. Encourage them to go back and revisit their goals and analyse what contributed to their success. Invite them to reflect on their learnings and make applications to their lives beyond the school gates, and their own futures.

The transference of learning to their life is often where the best learning happens.

Example questions for a class and buddy discussion include:

- What did you learn about working together?
- What did you discover about yourself as a learner?
- What did you do when you found others didn't agree with your ideas?
- How did you suppress your own desires and assume responsibility for achieving the group's goals?
- What new questions are you asking?
- What new insights have you gained that you can apply in the next project you work on?

- What did you do when you reached an impasse?
- How do you feel about your contribution to this project?
- What more could you have done?
- What experiences made you laugh?
- What did you learn about your use of the Habits of MInd? (see chapter 8)

Find out more about pondering and self-evaluation in chapter 4.

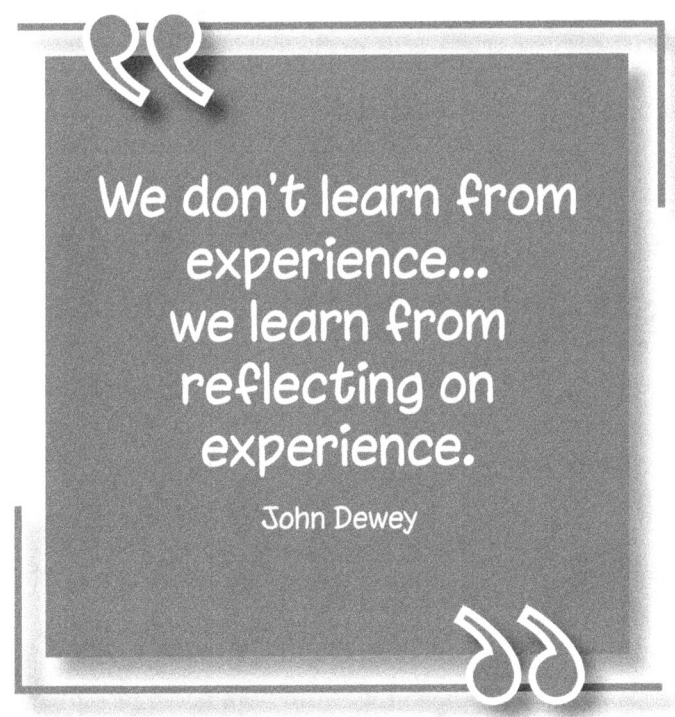

CHAPTER THREE

The Mechanics of How

After reading through the seven steps, there are likely to be many questions still circulating in your head. Here are some of the common questions I am asked about leading Genius Hour.

Time Frame

In general, a Genius Hour Project time will span ten weeks or less depending on the age of your students and the depth you want students to go into. Younger students might just do a 4-5 week variation. It is easier to contain the process within a term, rather than stretching it over the school holiday break as having to re-motivate students after a break can be challenging.

Most schools do this in the two middle terms of the year. The first term is usually focused on setting the routines and procedures in your classroom for the year, whilst the last term is often messy and shorter. This of course will depend on your students, your time frames and your experience with this process.

Genius Hour is generally 60 -90 minutes per week with a possible additional 30 minutes per week for the literacy side, writing the action plan, blogging, planning the pitch, presentations etc.

A 10 week process may look like this:

Week 1: An Introduction to Genius Hour: Students learn about the origins and purpose of Genius Hour and start to identify their interests and passions.
Step 1: Passion

Week 2: Generating Questions: Students generate their driving, inquiry questions and plan their proposed resources and timeline. A draft of the intended product and impact is completed.
Step 2: Plan

Week 3: The Approval: Students practice and give their pitch to the class or teacher.
Step 3: Pitch

Week 4: Research: Students start researching, contacting experts and implementing their plan.
Step 4: Project

Week 5: Research & Implementation: Students continue to implement their plan and record their results. They also reflect on their progress and make adjustments as required.
Step 4 & 5: Project & Product

Week 6: Research & Implementation: Students continue to implement their plan and record their results. They also reflect on their progress and make adjustments as required.
Step 4 & 5: Project & Product

Week 7: Implementation: Students continue to implement their plan and record their results. They also reflect on their progress and make adjustments as required.
Step 5: Product

Week 8: Implementation: Students continue to implement their plan and record their results. They also reflect on their progress and make adjustments as required.
Step 5: Product

Week 9: Complete the Product: Students compete their product and start developing their presentation.
Step 5 & 6: Product & Presentation

Week 10: Sharing: Students complete and practice their presentation and present at Presentation Day.

Step 6: Presentation

You may wish to schedule regular meetings with students to check on their progress and ensure they are on track.

At the start of each Genius Hour session, ask students to set goals of what they would like to achieve by the end of the session. This helps with focus and can increase productivity.

At the end of each Genius Hour session it is recommended to provide time for reflection and feedback. This helps students stay accountable as well as let others know how their class mates are progressing.

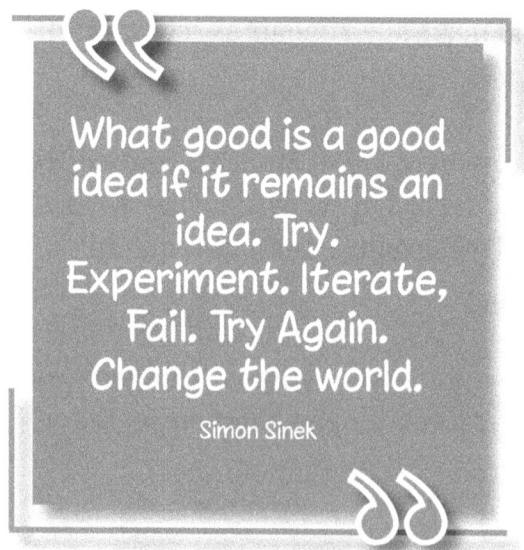

What good is a good idea if it remains an idea. Try. Experiment. Iterate, Fail. Try Again. Change the world.

Simon Sinek

Key Skills to Explicitly Teach

Throughout this process there will be key skills your students may need to be explicitly taught. These include:

- Research Skills: How to search online, how to use contents, index and print resources, note taking techniques, evaluating sources, citing sources...

- Organisational Skills: Keeping track of resources, creating and keeping deadlines, decision making, time managemen...

- Goal Setting & Planning Skills: Being specific, results oriented, realistic, recording...

- Inquiry Method: Formulate questions, exploring & investigate to find answers, build new understandings & meanings, share new knowledge, reflect and acting upon findings...

- Scientific method: Hypothesise, test, analyse, repeat...

- Speaking & listening skills: Team work, co-operation, written and oral communication...

The Role of the Teacher

What do you do over the 10 weeks? Your role is as a motivator, questioner and facilitator. The hardest part will be knowing when to leave students alone and when to step in.

Your role is not to provide the answers, or complete the task for them, nor are you expected to get the resources or clean-up for the students. This is their time and you are the guide on the side.

You will however have the opportunity to teach and reinforce skills and dispositions. This is likely to happen in real time and is not so easy to plan for. Students may need to learn how to make a phone call and script out their questions. They may require research support to stop them getting lost in the rabbit hole of the Internet. Students may need coaching on co-operation or assistance in learning how to compromise or incorporate others' ideas. They may possibly need reminders that this process is supposed to be hard, and that is where the learning truly happens. (There will be more). The list is extensive and will often surprise you to the simplicity and equally, the depth of teaching required. This is the really exciting part of project based learning. Genuine, authentic learning when students need it.

A brave (or maybe crazy?) teacher may choose to do their own Genius Hour project alongside the students. It is great opportunity to model the learning and share your epic failures. I know many teachers who have done this, and it is important to choose a genuine project – something you really want to learn, or an impact you want to make.

'Just in time' or the 'teachable moment' teaching will also occur. For instance, if a student needs to make a phone call, you may need to assist in writing a script as many students nowadays, do not know the etiquette or even the mechanic of how to make a phone call. They may need to script it and indeed role play it first. Similarly, students may not know how to write a letter, address an envelope or format an email.

You will not be able to plan for all the teachable opportunities, however you can pre-empt some. The key is for you to be as flexible as possible.

Motivation for Genius Hour Projects often becomes a challenge in the middle of the process, especially when students get stuck or things are not going to plan. In her book, *Raising Strong*, Brené Brown talks about the middle of any process is often messy. She refers to this as the 'Rumble' stage. She goes on to say this is where you must embrace the courage to learn, the courage to let go, ask questions of your assumptions, clarify expectations and ideas, and understand the situation and perspective of the situation, others and self.

CHAPTER FOUR

Assessment

A question often asked is, "How do I assess and evaluate a student's Genius Hour Project?" Opinion is mixed on this one.

Some teachers prefer not to create extra work load and stress in having to assess each student project and veterans in the process often comment that it is harder to access individual projects on a common set of criteria, especially – when the scope of what students do is so broad and unique. Others find there are certain parts of the process that can be assessed. The key here is the bigger purpose of the project based learning and the learning you want your students to experience. There may also be curriculum or learning areas you can link, such as oral presentations, research skills, writing skills and thinking dispositions.

Initially it might just be enough to guide students through the process and then create some evaluation rubrics and checklists. My preference is to co-create these with my students.

Assessment ideas may include:

- Originality of ideas
- Persistence & flexibility of thinking when stuck
- Completion of tasks in a timely manner
- Knowledge and expertise of subject
- Presentation skills

Once the criteria for assessment has been created, a great idea is to create book marks as a visual reminder for students.

Of course, there is a wonderful opportunity for students to conduct a self-evaluation of their project.

Self-Evaluation

Recorded presentations are wonderful for a self-evaluation. Usually this happens several weeks after the event to give students time to enjoy the glow of success and enough time to be slightly removed from the emotion of the presentation day.

Encourage students to be honest with their self-reflection as it is for them, to create more learning opportunities.

Key questions are useful for this:

- What was your key aim from your presentation?
- What did you want your audience to know, do or feel from your presentation?
- Did you achieve this?
- What went well with your presentation?
- What are some of the things you think you could have improved on?
- Did you follow the presentation structure – or get side tracked?
- What did you discover, observe or learn from watching yourself?
- What are some of your next learning steps?
- What are some of the things you might do differently next time?

Students may also evaluate the parts of the Genius Hour process. For example, you may have them reflect on their project, their team work, problem solving abilities, their presentation, the impact they wanted to make etc.

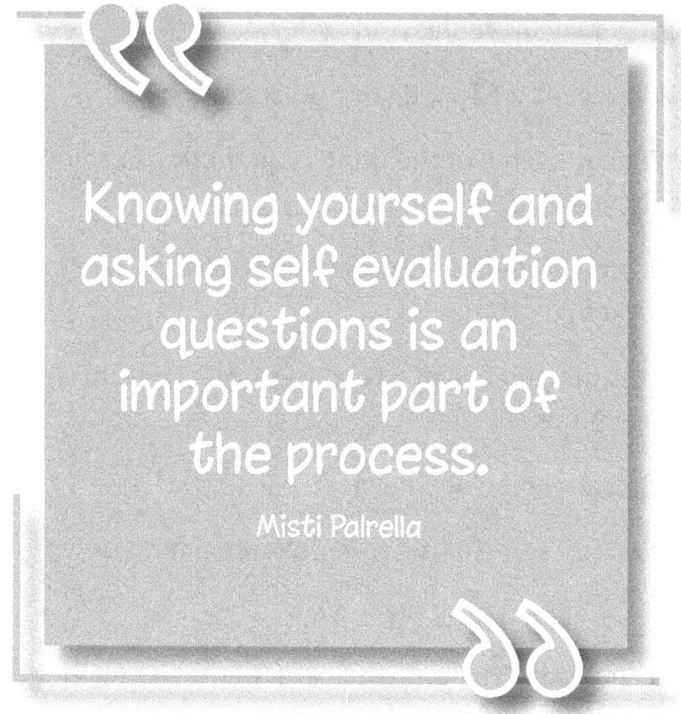

Knowing yourself and asking self evaluation questions is an important part of the process.

Misti Palrella

CHAPTER FIVE

Common Challenges

As with any initiative being implemented, there will always be challenges and learnings for a classroom teacher. It is the old adage, if you fail to plan, you are planning to fail. In saying this, there is an opportunity to learn from others who have been before.

Here are what other teachers have talked about...

- Ensure the problem is a rich problem with many angles of inquiry. It is important to create a problem which does not have a single answer. Enlist help from peers, parents, students and the community.

- Monitoring who is doing what. Planning clear milestones are key here. If students are working in pairs or small groups, it is important to ensure the division of labour is fair and students are not only working in their area of strength. Another challenge with working with a partner or sometimes alone, might be doing the minimum work. Again, setting expectations at the start of the project planning may help.

- Allow more time than you think you need for planning. This is a major key to the entire process and one that you will refine further as you become more experienced in the process.

- Explain the purpose and process clearly to parents. It is important for parents to understand Genius Hour is a deeper opportunity for learning. More about this in in chapter 7: Explaining to Parents.

- Avoid fundraising projects unless you have very clear systems and responsibilities around how the money will be accounted for and security for its storage.

- Let students fail. This is another fundamental key which has been mentioned by all teachers who have adopted Genius Hour in their classroom. It is part of the learning cycle and a wonderful opportunity for real world learning.

- Celebrate the risk taking. Again, an important tenant as students will be moving outside their comfort zones and challenging themselves, often beyond what they have done before. Celebrate the responsible risks they take and the use of drawing on their past knowledge. Here they will develop a sense of what is appropriate and an understanding about consequences of their thinking. To do this they will have to risk failure, which for many is a scary proposition.

- What if they do nothing during Genius Hour? This is a common question and concern. Discuss with students the idea of freedom come with responsibility. They are free to choose 'nothing' and the responsibility of that choice will be experienced at presentation time.

AJ Juliani suggests asking these students to help with your personal Genius Project, or to video the rest of the class in action. Maybe they could document the Genius Hour project as a mini documentary. They may 'catch' the enthusiasm of fellow students' passions in this process.

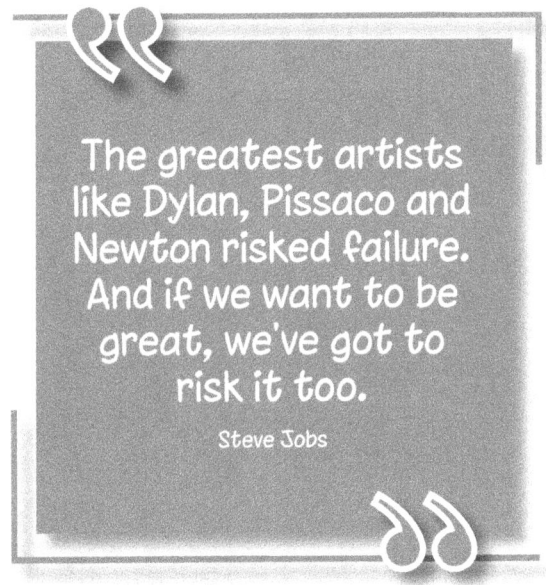

The greatest artists like Dylan, Pissaco and Newton risked failure. And if we want to be great, we've got to risk it too.

Steve Jobs

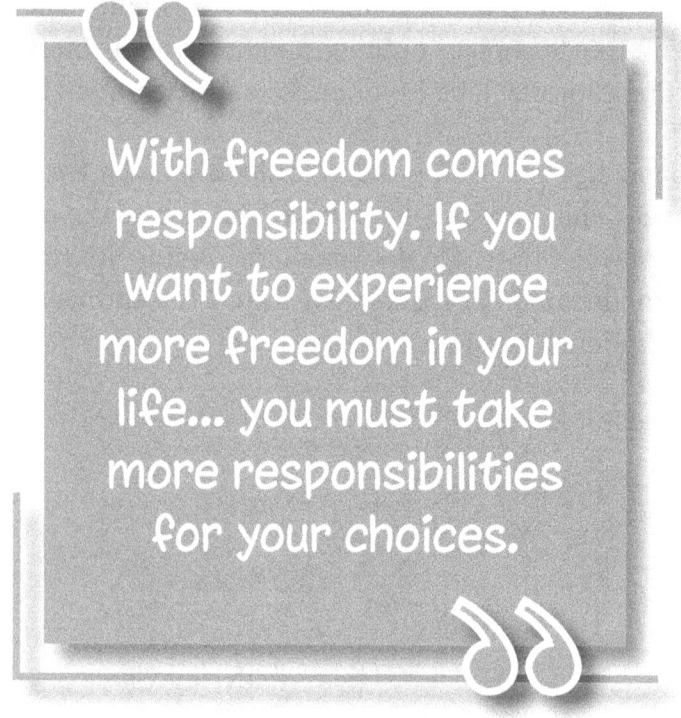

> With freedom comes responsibility. If you want to experience more freedom in your life... you must take more responsibilities for your choices.

CHAPTER SIX

Struggling Students

As exciting as Genius Hour sounds, some students struggle with aspects of this. Some will find it hard to get going each day and may require more guidance in the first few days and maybe throughout the Genius Hour process.

One such challenge can be finding a project.

Many students have spent their entire schooling being told what to do. When they are suddenly given choice and the freedom to choose they may well become overwhelmed with the prospect or indeed just not know how to choose.

Spend time with them to help find their passion of interest. Question them about their interests and what they like about it. Model for these students how their interests can be transformed into a project they care about and can get excited about. I once saw a teacher guide a student to do a project about how he could convince his Mum that playing online games was good for him!

At the back of this book you will find a list of project ideas, this might help spark some thoughts and possibilities.

The challenge of being given choice is for some learners it is a scary prospect. What if they choose wrong? What if they want to change half way? What if they see someone doing something they would rather do? Reassure them that choice can be challenging and it is the learning process not the end product that is the most important part.

Check in with your struggling students daily. They may need your guidance on where to start and how to gather and summarise information.

Allow your struggling students to do partner or small group projects. It is important they have clear roles, goals and milestones so the partner is not doing all the work.

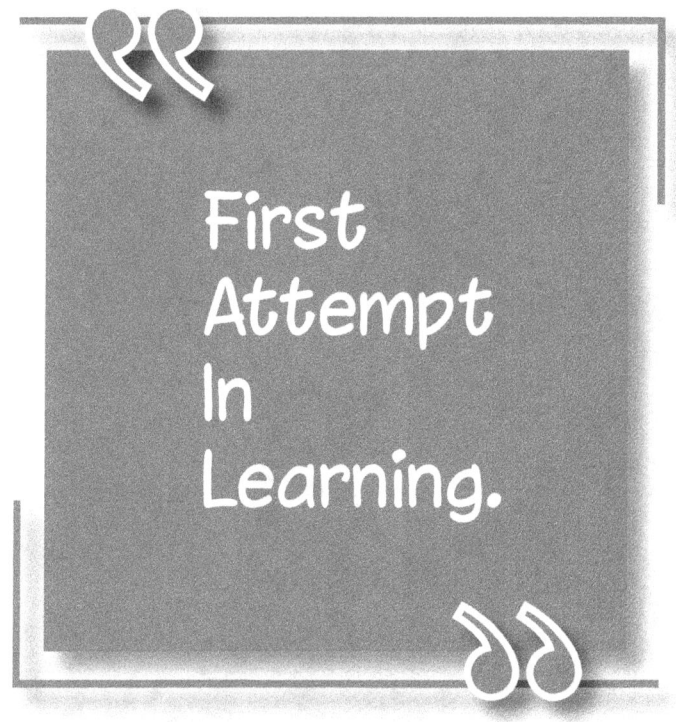

"First Attempt In Learning."

CHAPTER SEVEN

Explaining Genius Hour to Parents

Many parents have only experienced school from their own childhood and it was likely to have been very teacher directed. The 20th century school system was primarily set up to create employees – people who turned up on time, completed the tasks in a satisfactory manner, didn't question authority and clocked out at the end of the day.

In the 21st Century, with a world changing fast, known as the Information Age and moving into the Experience Age, the need for our students to embrace what are commonly called the 21st Century skills is imperative for their success.

The 21st Century skills include:

1. Critical thinking
2. Creativity
3. Collaboration
4. Communication
5. Information literacy
6. Media literacy
7. Technology literacy
8. Flexibility
9. Leadership
10. Initiative
11. Productivity
12. Social skills

Genius Hour provides a platform for students to learn many of these skills in a meaningful and authentic way, whilst also teaching students that they can have a positive impact on people, places and the planet.

It allows students to learn to take control of their learning by doing something that is their choice, combines their passions and interests, has a positive impact on this planet, and teaches students to be self-directed and independent.

Even more than that, students are very likely to encounter problems and challenges in their chosen project (in fact it is expected.) One of the goals of Genius Hour is for students to learn how to problem solve and develop strategies to move beyond the known and cope with the unknown. The key is to give students authentic experiences to learn what to do when they are stuck, and the answer is not immediately apparent.

Genius Hour also provides choice for students. Choice over learning increases their ownership, which in turn, engages students in their learning. Project based learning increases productivity and class morale. It is intended to spark curiosity, encourage lifelong learning, imagination, perseverance, self-awareness and adaptability.

The Learning Process

I also believe it is important parents know the learning journey and understand how the brain learns.

In a world with 'Helicopter' parents, hovering and overprotective, or 'Lawnmower' parents, who mow obstacles down so kids won't experience them in the first place, a conversation about allowing students to fail, learn teaching them to be independent and to be problem solvers may be necessary.

This includes sharing with parents that learning is a process and not always about the final outcome. Explain the concept of "Everything is hard before it is easy" and use analogies such as the process of their child learning to walk or ride a bike. They fell down many times to be successful. Learning involves falling over (or off) and getting back up. Show concepts and posters on how mistakes are an important parent of the learning process.

One of my favourite analogies is to talk about the butterfly. If you help it out of the chrysalis or cocoon, it will die. It is the struggle that strengthens the wings and allows it to fly. The same is true with our children. The struggle builds the learning muscles, the resilience to cope with further challenges.

Delaying Gratification

Another great concept to share is the Marshmallow test. The marshmallow experiment was a series of studies in the late 1960's on the effects of delayed gratification, by Stanford psychologist Walter Mischel. Young children were given a choice between one small reward provided immediately (usually a marshmallow) or two small rewards if they waited for 10-15 minutes, during which the researcher left the room. Follow-up studies found that children who were able to wait longer for the extra rewards tended to have higher standardised test scores, and better educational attainment.

Although higher test scores is not the only measure of success for our students, the study showed the importance of students being able to delay gratification. This is a key component in success, as you have to do the hard work, before the rewards come. Genius Hour parallels this beautifully. It is often hard, messy and sometimes frustrating, teaching students to be able to manage their impulses and put the work in to get the success.

The Power of Influence

One of the desires of the many students I have worked with, is to feel they have purpose and can lead a meaningful life. The process of Genius Hour shows them they can influence the world and make a positive contribution. One such inspiration is Christopher Evans from Florida. I met Christopher in 2018 and had the pleasure of interviewing him. At just 10 years old, he has made a huge impact by fundraising with a lemonade stand over the past four years. Yes, he started when he was six! He has been instrumental in building three homes for villagers in Haiti. These houses saved the lives of villagers during Hurricane Matthew in 2016. Christopher's motto is, "You are never too young or old to make a difference!" You can follow him on social media #urnevertooyoung.

Time Management

One of the biggest learnings and conversations students have during and after their Genius Hour projects is about time management. Often students make their goals and aspirations of what they can achieve in a ten week block, far too big, or challenging and one of the consequences of this is that they learn about managing their time and expectations.

Involve Parents

One of the best ways to get parent engagement is to involve them as experts, advisors and helpers during Genius Hour.

Advertise the need for experts in the areas required, or even better, invite students to write or call parents or community members to assist when they are able. Grandparents can be perfect for this as well. They often have the skills and time to help during a school day.

It is important to speak to helpers about not 'doing' the project for the student, however being the guide on the side, the advisor, teacher and the safety eyes for projects which require it.

CHAPTER EIGHT

Underlying Assumptions

Before you launch into Genius Hour, it is useful to take a step back to see what the underlying assumptions are, and whether your students have the skills to be successful in project based learning. Of course, not all your students may have all of these skills, and indeed, Genius Hour is a wonderful opportunity to teach and reinforce such skills.

These strategies and skills can be the focus in the first term or half semester before your launch into Genius Hour. Addressing and teaching these underlying assumptions will give your students a stronger grounding for Genius Hour.

Independence

To be successful in any project based learning opportunity students will be required to work independently. They will be required to be self-managing to find, bring, access and organise resources. Self-management requires being able to stay on task and focused for sustained periods of time and knowing how to interact appropriately with others around them. Being able to manage their time is also a necessary skill here. Students will also need to be self-monitoring. This means they can self-evaluate where they are at in the process and choose options for their next steps. This is also about self- awareness of their own skills, abilities, strengths and weaknesses.

Collaboration

Working with others, sharing the tasks and responsibilities, as well as the outcome is a life skill and an important one to consider before students launch into group or partner projects.

Ensure you have spent time clearly teaching co-operation skills, team work and communication tools. I highly recommend the Kagan Co-operative Structures for this. Check out their offerings at www.kaganonline.com.

The Learning Process

During this process, the learning opportunities might be at times overwhelming. It is one of the great joys and frustrations of Genius Hour! Knowing the learning process is valuable for your students to be able to understand their journey.

Learning has many layers: It involves working through the hard to get to easy, being aware of the learning pit, feeling uncomfortable, consciously choosing strategies to help when it is challenging, repetition, metacognition, having a purpose – a big why, mindset, seeing the big picture and so many more facets.

Here are a few of my favourites to teach...

Growth Mindset

Carol Dweck, Stanford University psychologist speaks and writes about mindset in relationship to success and achievement. She advocates there are two types. A fixed mindset and a growth mindset.

People with a fixed mindset believe that their intelligence or talents are fixed – and success happens or it doesn't, depending on their intelligence. People with a growth mindset believe their basic qualities can be developed with effort, focus, training, coaching and hard work.

This table outlines some of the key differences ...

A FIXED Mindset Person...	A GROWTH Mindset Person...
Believes intelligence is something you are born with	Believes intelligence comes from hard work and can always improve
Tends to give up easily when faced with a challenge	Embraces challenges as an opportunity to grow
Sees effort as unnecessary and something you do if you are not good enough	Sees effort as essential and as a path to mastery
May take offense to feedback and often takes it personally	Uses feedback as something to learn from and to improve
Blames others and gets discouraged with setbacks	Uses setbacks as an opportunity to work harder next time

Developing a growth mindset is essential for success. A growth mindset means students develop a love of learning and resilience. Carol Dweck suggests teaching a growth mindset creates motivation and productivity in business, education and sports. She says it also enhances relationships.

Genius Hour is an ideal opportunity to reinforce and deepen students' growth mindset.

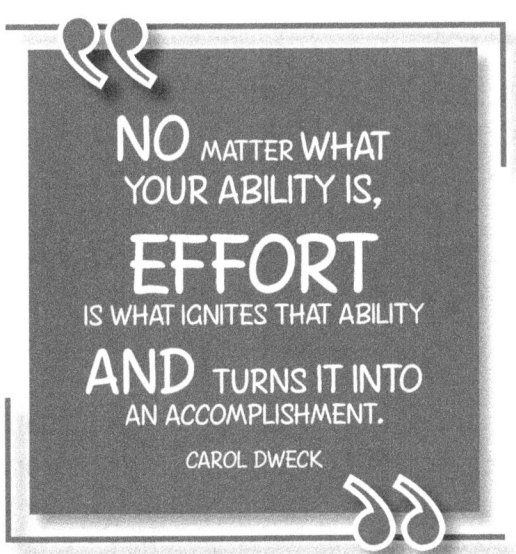

> NO MATTER WHAT YOUR ABILITY IS, EFFORT IS WHAT IGNITES THAT ABILITY AND TURNS IT INTO AN ACCOMPLISHMENT.
>
> CAROL DWECK

A key strategy in doing this is when praising students. Praise their effort, concentration, strategies and give specific feedback. Comments such as "Your persistence really paid off in completing your work today" is far more effective than "great work." The pivotal element is to praise repeatable behaviours. Just telling a student that they are a 'good boy/girl' or 'amazing' is not repeatable as they often do not know what they did to be 'good' or 'amazing.' Instead use phrases such as: "Taking the time to go back and check your work has produced a great result." "Wow, you really stopped to think about your challenge and have implemented changes to ensure a successful outcome." "Outstanding effort in focusing on your task today." As a teacher, reflect on the praise you often hear yourself giving. Is it the effort or final result that you are acknowledging?

Everything is Hard Before it is Easy

"To get to easy you have to go through hard." This was a soft drink commercial on the back of a bus and on billboards in Wellington, New Zealand.

A great Genius Hour project is going to stretch and challenge students beyond what they have done before. And it is going to get hard.

Many times students have been sold on the fact that learning is fun. It is not always! Sometimes it is uncomfortable, awkward and that feeling of potential failure is something most of us like to avoid, however this is exactly what learning new and unfamiliar content feels like. When learning becomes hard, many people give up. Again the key is, as the advert says, "To get to easy, you have to go through hard."

I believe we have a huge responsibility as teachers to ensure our children know that life can be hard, that they will fail and that life can be unfair.

When students are stuck or just don't know what to do, it is useful to have anticipated this and have discussed, practiced and reinforced what they can do at this point. This is part of teaching independence and self-management. The last thing you need is 26 students, working on individual projects, all asking you to help them through the hard.

In life, we often start on our journey with a goal in mind, a plan of perfection and in reality the journey is frequently very bumpy. It is, however in those bumps, those challenging times, where the best learning often happens.

Many teachers are facing students suffering from learned helplessness in their classrooms. They are paralysed with fear of failing and making mistakes. It is in the making of mistakes, the failing, the bumpiness, where life feels unfair. Teach students they have a working brain and a functioning body and always have choices when faced with challenges.

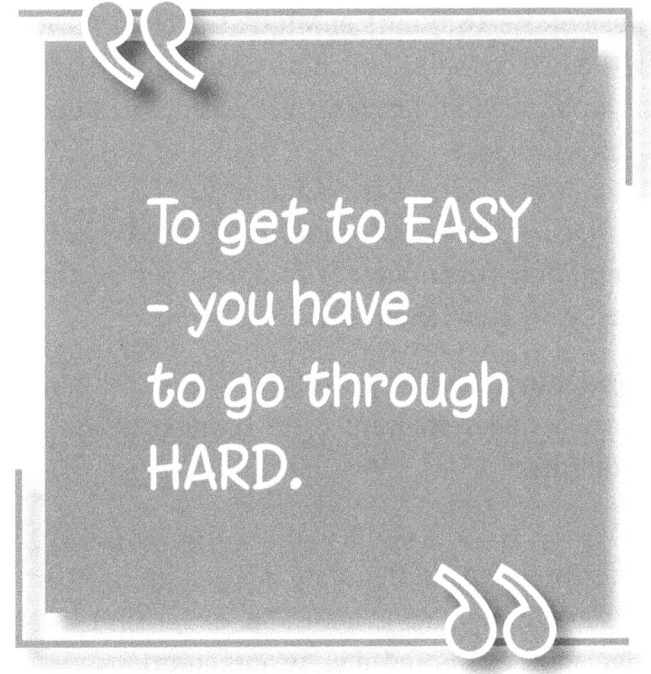

To get to EASY - you have to go through HARD.

Getting Unstuck

When students find themselves stuck and not sure what to do, teach them how to persist, try again and keep going. If plan A doesn't work there are 25 more letters in the alphabet!

Two people who have thought a great deal about this, are Professor Art Costa and Dr Bena Kallick. They studied, founded and developed the 16 Habits of Mind. These are the behaviours of intelligent people and what they do when they are stuck, the answer is not immediately apparent and they are not sure how to move from the hard to the easy.

A summary of the 16 Habits of Mind are below. As you read through the list, consider which dispositions or Habits your students would benefit learning from before and during the Genius Hour Process.

1. **Persisting:** *Stick to it!* Persevering in task through to completion; remaining focused. Looking for ways to reach your goal when stuck. Not giving up.

2. **Managing Impulsivity:** *Take your time!* Thinking before acting; remaining calm, thoughtful and deliberative.

3. **Listening with Understanding and Empathy:** *Understand others!* Devoting mental energy to another person's thoughts and ideas; Making an effort to perceive another's point of view and emotions.

4. **Thinking Flexibly:** *Look at it another way!* Being able to change perspectives, generating alternatives, considering options.

5. **Thinking about Thinking (Metacognition):** *Know your knowing!* Being aware of your own thoughts, strategies, feelings and actions and their effects on others.

6. **Striving for Accuracy:** *Check it again!* Always doing your best. Setting high standards. Checking and finding ways to improve constantly.

7. **Questioning and Posing Problems:** *How do you know?* Having a questioning attitude; knowing what data are needed & developing questioning strategies to produce those data. Finding problems to solve.

8. **Applying Past Knowledge to New Situations:** *Use what you learn!* Accessing prior knowledge; transferring knowledge beyond the situation in which it was learned

9. **Thinking and Communicating with Clarity and Precision:** *Be clear!* Striving for accurate communication in both written and oral form; avoiding over-generalisations, distortions, deletions and exaggerations.

10. **Gathering Data through All Senses:** *Use your natural pathways!* Paying attention to the world around you.

Gathering data through all the senses. taste, touch, smell, hearing and sight.

11. **Creating, Imagining, Innovating:** *Try a different way!* Generating new and novel ideas, fluency, originality

12. **Responding with Wonderment and Awe:** *Have fun figuring it out!* Finding the world awesome, mysterious and being intrigued with phenomena and beauty.

13. **Taking Responsible Risks:** *Venture out!* Being adventuresome; living on the edge of one's competence. Try new things constantly.

14. **Finding Humour:** *Laugh a little!* Finding the whimsical, incongruous and unexpected. Being able to laugh at one's self.

15. **Thinking Interdependently:** *Work together!* Being able to work in and learn from others in reciprocal situations. Team work.

16. **Remaining Open to Continuous Learning:** *Learn from experiences!* Having humility and pride when admitting we don't know; resisting complacency.

Obviously, these Habits are lifelong learning tools which are important whether you are engaging in the Genius Hour projects or not. These behaviours can be taught explicitly to students.

Brainstorm with students a list of strategies to employ when they are stuck and are faced with hard and difficult. It is a great idea to have these listed on a poster and regularly remind students that there are many options to help them get unstuck, rather than just calling upon the teacher.

For more information please go to www.instituteforhabitsofmind.com

The Learning Pit

James Nottingham's concept of the learning pit is a helpful one during the Genius Hour process. It gives students a structure and language to explain their frustrations within the learning process and identifies steps that help them out of the pit. James advocates for teachers to design learning experiences that cause students to be 'in the pit' and therefore induce learning.

In a nutshell, students fall into the 'learning pit' when they are unsure, stuck and working on challenging information that is hard, unexpected or new. This often creates feelings of wanting to quit, frustration, 'it's too hard" and not understanding what they are doing. Falling into this 'pit' is exactly where students do some of their best learning!

When students know they are 'in the pit' they can take steps to work out how to get themselves (or accept help from others) out of the pit. This is when the Habits of Mind really come to the fore. Strategies and Habits such as persisting, thinking flexibly, metacognition, taking responsible risks and so on will assist to pull students out of the confusion, support problem solving and facilitate a more successful outcome.

Responsibility Framework

A framework that I have used to help understand personal responsibility is below.

A question I often ask is, "Are you playing above or below the line?" or "Are you playing in the Victim team or the Learning team?"

In a nutshell, it helps students see if their comments, behaviour and self-talk is helping them learn or not. When 'playing below the line' people will often blame, make excuses and deny their actions, mistakes, outcomes, etc. This causes them to miss out on the learning opportunity from that situation. Below the line comments include:

- It was his fault
- I haven't got time
- I had nothing to do with it
- This is stupid

Students who 'play above the line,' look for the learning opportunity by taking ownership of their results, become accountable for their actions and responsible for their outcomes. Above the line comments include:

- I made a mistake and need to fix that
- I hurt my partner's feelings by not listening fully and need to apologise
- I didn't express my ideas and am not happy with the direction we are going. I need to call a team meeting
- It's my fault for not managing my time well

We are all human and it is normal to blame, make excuses and deny. The critical factor is that when students recognise they are below the line, they can reframe the challenge or situation from the position of the learning team - above the line. This is about letting students know that they always have choice when they are faced with a challenging situation or having made a mistake.

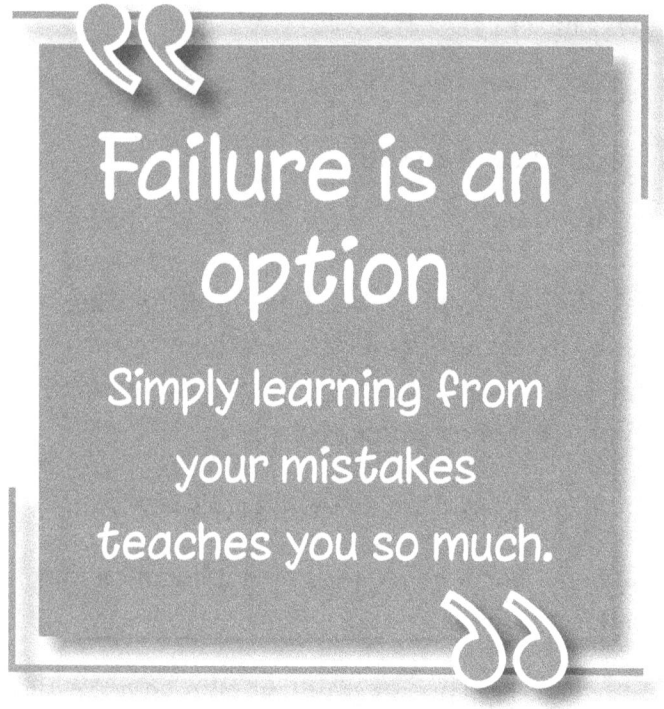

CHAPTER NINE

Final Thoughts

Before I leave you in the hands of five teachers who have implemented Genius Hour in their classrooms, I want you to know the truth about leading Genius Hour. You will never be fully prepared to lead the process. There is so much scaffolding, and so many elements your students may need to learn, and dive in anyway. Have fun. Be flexible. Expect the unexpected. Hold the space for your students to create, lead and experience great learning. If you don't know how to help them, be up front and explain your frustrations and unknowingness. Enrol students to help come up with solutions to the challenges. Be a model of the learning process.

Once you have a handle on Genius Hour, modify this process as much as you need. In fact, I expect it! Remember to keep the big picture of individual learning in mind.

This is an opportunity to allow your students to express themselves, to develop lifelong learning skills, be curious, find their passions and strengths.

Most of all, please share your student success stories with the world, let them know they can make a difference, show them the impact they have, and as Christopher Evans says, you are never too young or old!

Part Two
Practical Ideas From the Classroom

CHAPTER TEN

A Game Changer
Simon Ashby

Genius Hour can be a game changer in your classroom because it allows you to see your students in a new light, sometimes casting light where you only saw darkness. The responsibility for student achievement relies solely on the shoulders of the student themselves which can often be first experience of either success or failure for that child. This can be an empowering exercise and it can also be excruciatingly painful at times. In my opinion, the gains far exceed any pain you or students may suffer for the best learning happens when the learner takes charge. Students should be central in the learning process not bystanders in yours.

Students love Genius Hour for obvious reasons. We are allowing students the freedom to learn what they want to learn and to be proud of their own innate skills. We are showing students that school is an exciting place to be. It helps to promote school as a place that they belong to, is relevant and it promotes self efficacy.

When we allow our students to be creative and think for themselves it also requires teachers to let go of certainties. The privilege of teaching is that every day is different. In the 21st Century every year seems different-trying to keep up with technological change is near impossible. We as teachers need to be comfortable with being uncomfortable. We live in an era of unprecedented change. Where the knowledge of the world can be contained within your pocket. What we need to create is a culture where it's OK for your learners to learn alongside you and perhaps know even more than you do. And so school needs to be relevant for our learners because relevancy is the key to retention. Our job is to provide students with what David Theriault coins as 'sticky' memories-make learning memorable, magic, a happening. Genius Hour is one way in which you can teach students can create their own story, to go from being a consumer of learning to a creator.

In the era of student agency, it is also a simple and practical way to take your first dip into student choice and voice. In our school where Genius Hour is now normalised, my students (aged 7-8) are not afraid of the concept. However, when we first started on our journey, the concept of a child devising, planning, researching, creating everything was a risky and exciting prospect. My colleagues were on board from the start which has been amazing. However, I can imagine in a school where you are on your own the risk will fall at your feet. Let me reassure you and scare you at the same time. You will bask in the glory of many of your students creating wonderful and weird projects that they look back on for many years with pride. Parents will love the concept and come willingly to your sharing afternoons because they will have heard non stop about it from their proud and engaged child. Your principal will love you for it because those same parents will tell you Principal what a wonderful teacher you are for allowing your students to be so engaged. Some of your colleagues will 'click' with the concept and want your advice. You've become the expert and the now the cycle continues.

Genius Hour can flop if you let it, however. You need to work hard behind the scenes to motivate and explain the 'why' behind what you are attempting. Don't take anything for granted. It would be easy to assume that certain kids will knock this out of the park and others won't. Genius Hour brings out the best in most and the worst in some children. So keep on top of where people are and what they've been up to. Though you are placing great trust in them to get the job done, you still need to keep them accountable for their time and productivity.

Being In Flow

In my classroom I talk a lot about being in the zone, in your happy place. Think about it, when you are in the zone, time passes quickly, it is absorbing. The opposite is also true. Time passes so slowly when we are engaged with a task that you find boring (like meeting with the bank manager). We need to help students build a deep love of learning as the first and most important objective of schooling. All else can flow on from having a motivated and curious learner. You are showing your students that what matters to them, matters to you, matters full stop. Learners are empowered when they are allowed the freedom to complete learning tasks that come from them. Teach your students to value the things important to them. Be it dance, poetry, painting, writing, football, coding, conservation. Teach them that the most innovative thing that they can do in life is to be themselves.

Knowing and Discovering Your Learners

However, in your heart of hearts, you know there is that child who will struggle. You know the one. Not that one! The one that finds school easy, that coasts and loves praise. He or she makes great posters. They always have an answer and love their times tables. Mum and Dad come in to look at their books regularly and always turn up to parent teacher night, sometimes with a written list of questions. How does a child that loves structure, praise and rules adapt to an open concept of learning? Well firstly, they don't. They need to be told a few things-privately.

Firstly, Genius Hour is going to be the hardest thing they've ever done. Secondly, it's OK not to know what to do, how to do it, what your passion is etc. Thirdly, Genius Hour is an opportunity to extend themselves beyond what you (and they) thought possible. I say to them, if they know what the outcome of their project is form the start then what was the point? A strong project requires adaptation, changing your mind, trying new things. Fourthly, as your teacher, I'm more than happy to suggest some areas for you to go down, but the ultimate decision is yours.

There are a couple of other children to know about. The first brings me great joy, because these children have plastic brains that cope with setbacks. Ultimately, they are also very organised. These are your go getters, who I kid you not, will require very little input from you once they are up and running. These children will delight and astonish you with what weird and wonderful creation they make. They will surprise you at every turn by remembering their materials, having pre sawed some wood with Mum on the weekend, brought glue from Grandad and sewn on teddy eyes before school that morning. They will be resolutely proud of what they've done regardless of how it looks, because they did it themselves. This I estimate to be from anywhere between 50-90% of your class.

Finally, you have your "dunno" children. Idealistic teacher: "What are you interested in learning about?" "Dunno". "What do you do on the weekend? "Not much" etc. When you take your time to bore down into these children's lives I've often found the "dunno" comes from fear of failure or standing out too much from fear of bullying etc. It may be cliche, but the best projects I've found for these children are usually hands on. Building, designing, filming, creating. Our brilliant Caretaker has been known to take some under his wing and help a pipe dream become a reality. These children require simply, a poke or prod in the right direction, some structure to support them, the freedom to fail and lots of check ins from you. A good chunk of your class really won't need you as much anymore, because they're fine. They've got themselves under control. Really. Take the time to work alongside "dunno" and find out what they are good at, curious about, want to be good at etc.

I can't promise Genius Hour will instantly turn around this child's life or circumstances. What I have witnessed however, time and again is an increased desire to come to school, an increased motivation in other areas of school and often, but not always, that blessed question, "What day is Genius Hour again Mr?" This is for the simple reason that even for you most "dunnoest" child in the world, Genius Hour has become the best part of school for them.

Out of the Box

The best learning happens in the minds and souls of individuals, not on worksheets and tests. Which parts of the curriculum do schools willingly neglect to their own detriment? As Sir Ken Robinson points out, why do we prioritise reading, writing and maths so strongly over the arts? Musicians John Lennon and Paul McCartney both hated school but found themselves through their passions. How many countless students do we know of that do not fit the traditional school mould of teaching and learning? We need to switch our classes from a control narrative to a passion based narrative. In the past we have rewarded compliance not initiative because that is what is easiest to measure. Schelcty's model of engagement asks are students engaged with the task at hand or just strategically complying because they know that's the way to get ahead? It is our job as teachers not to make students fit in our box, but to adjust what are doing to meet the needs of the individual. The problem being of course is that making the box is easy, it's tidy and people can see it.

Genius Hour is thusly, messy and untamed. It is not a pretty box that you open and close away. Your classroom will

become a sea of cardboard pieces, hot glue will seep into carpet and popsicle sticks will haunt your dreams. That being said, how can you prepare the space to allow your students to be successful? Can you create spaces in your room that are hotbeds of gluing and making, spaces for dancing and filming...a makerspace....a choreography space...a music space....a quiet writing space...a taking cardboard boxes apart then leaving the bits everywhere space. Ask for suggestions from your learners about how to make your learning space work best during Genius Hour? Ask them what would they like to make it work for them, not the other way around.

Freedom Is Hard

Being told what to do, though not exciting, is easy. When asked to learn what they wanted to learn, some of my children didn't know what to do. The asked me what their passion was. Some children find it hard to recognise their own talents or passion. How can we help those children who do not recognise their own passions or have a burning desire to learn something new?

We need to create a culture that lets students fail. From the first day of school, let your students know that it's ok to take risks in your class. That failure is an option. Find the key concept for your class and set the tone. It may be, the love of learning, curiosity, risk taking, whatever, whenever, set a hopeful and positive tone for the year.

Give them time. Let them change their minds. Share previous projects from around the globe. Make it OK to sit on an idea for a while. But teach them to change their minds quickly. 'Fail fast' we say. Don't drag out your failure, get it over with quickly. Celebrate a culture of trial and error learning. Let students create numerous prototypes. Failure teaches our learners to tweak the formula and create a better version, a more considered and meaningful experience. By nature, innovation and creativity should always be a work in progress.

If we are to pursue anything valuable in life, it means you have to be willing to fail. Ask any student if they would ever keep playing or recommend a computer game they clocked on the first round! As a teacher, if your lesson went perfectly to plan, the first time, was it really worth learning? When your students know that they aren't going to be punished for trial and error learning, then they do begin to push their own boundaries further.

If one of your students picks something that is very, very, very big and ambitious do not ever doubt them, just let them be free and do what they want to do". (Amy, 10)

Thusly, we need to have faith and believe in the innate abilities of our students.

The Balance of Creativity & Deadlines

A common dilemma is how to encourage students to be creative and yet also stick to a deadline? One strength of having a deadline is that students get to practise using time. It allows them to be in control of time. It is very rare to find a student off task during Genius Hour. Confused and frustrated definitely. Some students will find the freedom too much the first time around and fail to finish with much to show for themselves. Some lack organisational skills and can require reminders the first time you attempt Genius Hour.

Therefore, it is critical you stick to deadlines and give plenty of reminders about time management. The second try at Genius Hour is always far stronger as the students have learnt how to use their time best. I have found my students will come to school early to work on their projects and also at home involving their parents in the process.

Shout From The Roof Tops - A Star Is Born

Move over fake news, Genius Hour speaks the truth! Genius Hour is a publicity beast. A starlet that deserves to be in all the photos. Believe the hype, Genius Hour is coming and it wants to be plastered on your classroom's windows, all over the doors, in the hallways. Hey, your newsletter needs a cover page, who better to ask than Genius Hour? Your class blog, site or seesaw should be unashamedly plastered with Genius Hour propaganda. Firstly, your parents need to know what this thing is their kid suddenly wants 400 popsicle sticks for. Secondly, your colleagues who are on the fringe of giving it a go will benefit from seeing your propaganda photos of students winning. Why not hit the staff car park with flyers advertising your classes sharing day? Thirdly, if you are plastering Genius Hour everywhere then it is without doubt going to benefit your learners who are already proud as punch, to see themselves in the school office, the Principal's office, the school Facebook page is just another leg up that they deserve.

Share with the world. Let your learners know that their contribution to the world is important and value it as such. Ask your students what ways they think they could make their project go big or viral even. My students utilise my Youtube channel, connect via my teacher twitter account, contact local journalists, skype experts in, email interested and or affected parties...for example the CEO of whatever company might like their ideas. Can they connect with other children around the world? Invite the whole school community to come in and ask the hard questions at the end of the project. This helps drive student accountability and your students will love the attention. My students blog regularly about their Genius Hour projects. This helps make learning more visible.

Genius Hour, should ask you also to consider what other aspects of your classroom programme need more student choice. Once your students have a taste of choice and freedom they are going to want more. Are you ready for the challenge? More to the point, are you willing to take that opportunity?

Other Considerations

- Technology can play a major part in a successful project and it can be a distraction. These are handy teaching points for you to navigate. Technology however, needs to be ubiquitous for our 21st century learners. They should have the freedom to choose the most appropriate tool to research, design and present their learning.

- Don't assign marks, instead place the emphasis on self-reflection and peer feedback. Most of my learners say the feedback they get from whanau and peers is one of the highlights of the whole process.

- Let students have a learning journal or place of reflection which provides evidence of learning when things go pear shaped, and place to record ideas and inspiration, doodles etc.

- Let students come to the idea themselves, no matter how hard they push you for it. Help lead them through a good brainstorming session, but their projects will be so much stronger for having come from themselves.

- Adventure together. Be OK with not knowing everything for your students. Keep learning and innovating yourself and make this innovation visible with your learners. Let your students know how you are constantly experimenting, failing, learning also. Be explicit that you are attempting something new with Genius Hour and need their help and participation to help it work. That you would like feedback on Genius Hour and that you too can fail fast and learn from your mistakes as well.

- Take photos every session of every student. These will prove invaluable at sharing time.

Feel the fear and do it anyway

Psychologist C.D Ryuff has found that engaging adolescents in learning helps to develop their personal sense of worth and belonging, which fosters: a heightened sense of freedom, a decrease in the fear of failure, an increase in self-worth, the ability to take more risks, an increase in independence and more self-kindness when mistakes occur. This is the kind of human flourishing we as educators are surely paid to give damn about. Let's let our learners recognise that what matters to them, matters to you. That it's not what we provide for our learners, but what we allow them to try to do and teach them to do for themselves that will mould them into successful human beings.

Simon Ashby is a Year ¾ teacher in Nelson. He is a Google Certified Innovator and Trainer. His passions lie in digital, environmental and arts education. Genius Hour has been a classroom staple and saviour for over 6 years.

Contact @SimonAshbyNZ on Twitter.

CHAPTER ELEVEN

A Rite of Passage
Miriam Bell

When I first embarked on my classroom Genius Hour journey 5 years ago, it was fraught with the fear of the dreaded 'what ifs...' What if my students spent an entire term wandering about and creating nothing but mess? What if the classroom climate degenerated into raucous hotbed of chaos? What if parents or my teaching partners questioned its value or aren't on board? What if the children produced terrible ideas?

The result of this near-crippling plague of doubt was that I was forced to create systems and strategies to deal with the 'what ifs' when they strike. And strike they do, because Genius Hour by its very nature is messy, frustrating, noisy, and not particularly measurable in terms of specific learning outcomes. It flies in the face of targeted acceleration programmes and tiered achievement modules. It can, however, be exactly the thing that sparks joy in the school day for many students, and can be the ultimate link to real-life learning that crosses the boundaries between home and school, or student and teacher.

The process that we follow in our classroom varies term by term, but it has become entrenched as a rite of passage in our school. Younger students talk to me in the playground about their theories regarding what they see the seniors working on, and Year 7s start unpacking ideas with me before I've even got my head around the maths programme for the year. It has become a beast that I couldn't shake off even if I wanted to!

Initially, my overthinking and determination that every child would achieve greatness simultaneously created an enormous amount of stress for me as a teacher, and probably for the children as well. My micromanaged charts, learning logs, feedback modules, workshops, and showcases were effective in that they produced many great projects. They also pushed some students beyond where they were ready to go, and drove me (and no doubt a few parents) halfway up the wall. Over the past few years, I've tried to find a balance for all of us.

What do you value?

As a teacher, Genius Hour is exhausting. It clearly underlines the weaknesses in your classroom management and the gaps in your instruction. The rewards however, are myriad. Enabling students of all academic abilities to follow their passions, create something they value, and reflect intelligently on their growth, make this concept incredibly worthwhile.

Clear scaffolding is vital to ensure that children are aware of expectations and have something to frame their thinking. They need to know their work has a purpose. They need to be accountable. They also need to know that failure is a crucial part of the learning process. Students have to develop resilience when their project falters and perseverance when their initial passion wanes. Which it will. Possibly multiple times. This stuff is the engine that drives the powerful learning that is Genius Hour.

It has become important to me in recent years that students have the opportunity to work towards something beyond themselves. They are encouraged to ask themselves how their learning can create an impact on a local or global level. This is usually linked to concepts that we have explored in class or events that have captured the media. Often this has led to enterprise type projects, where things of value are created and sold, and the money spent on something for specific community groups or charities. It may simply be a

the creation of a tool through which they can educate people about their passions or wider issues, such as a podcast, or website.

Project Examples

After meeting a local family with a young child who has battled cancer, some of my students became interested in creating 'Chemo Kits' for children and their families in Christchurch's Children's Haematology Oncology Centre. This involved much research into immunity, microbe exposure, and discussions around how an illness can impact on family dynamics and mental health. The girls ran a sausage sizzle at the local Warehouse, went shopping, and created 10 absolutely beautiful bags full of toys and activities appropriate for children and their families who were spending extended time isolated in hospital. Delivering these with the children who created them was a true career highlight for me.

One year, during a school focus on Kaitiakitanga, a group of children became passionate about the decline of native bird species due to stoats and rats. Their interest led them to design and build traps, which led them to debate the ethics around pest extermination, revise their trap design to line  up with DOC guidelines, make more traps, and excitedly set them under DOC supervision around our local area. There was huge excitement when an enormous rat was caught breaking and entering a local chicken coop!

Another group of children became concerned about the mental health of the elderly in a local rest home. They undertook some research groundwork and decided to learn some card games and magic tricks that they could play and share with the residents. It was truly wonderful to watch this rambunctious collection of boys practicing their euchre skills on the picnic tables during lunchtime at school, and they brought many smiles and tears on their visits to the rest home facility, where they did as much talking and listening as they did card playing.

Archie and Otto converted a remote controlled car to operate on solar power. This was a project that required 3 pitches

 to get off the ground, as their initial idea was vague, as was their understanding of solar energy. The amount of learning that took place was huge, but it took a great deal of strategic questioning and redirection to get there.

 Ella and Ribh designed and built a scale model of a live-in horse float, using tiny house design principles. This was another huge undertaking that caused a lot of initial frustration as they realised the intricates involved with vehicle sizes and practical space saving. The end product was very cool!

Of course not all students are entirely altruistic, and service is not an essential part of my Genius Hour programme. It's interesting to note however, that all of these particular projects stemmed from various class conversations about uncomfortable issues. Children on the whole are naturally optimistic, and reframing the difficult stuff into 'so what can we do about it?' is empowering for all of us, wherever it may lead.

Timetabling

In recent years, I've moved away from a whole class Genius Hour focus. There have been many reasons for this, but my sanity was the main one. Our topic work is largely project-based by nature these days, using various matrices of work options based on particular themes that we are exploring as a class. Within this, there are knowledge-based workshops and optional tasks and activities that accrue points. When a certain amount of points have been accrued, Genius Hour presents itself as an option for those that wish to pursue it. They are required to follow a particular process to streamline their thinking and maximise their learning. Those that aren't yet inspired can choose to continue with their other topic learning, accruing more points or embarking on another phase of learning, depending on the topic at the time.

This timetabling tweak has proved beneficial in a number of ways. For starters, the children with big ideas get on with it and underway, inspiring those who haven't yet developed a vision. It also staggers the chaos, meaning that you have fewer corners to dash between while the projects are underway. It also works well in both a single cell and innovative learning environment, as long as all parties take the time to plan their roles and time for the next session.

A few students choose not to take part in Genius Hour, which initially I found disappointing. Over time, however, my observation has been that these children are often just more cautious learners. They may attempt it on a later cycle, after they have ironed out any concerns that they may have regarding their own ability to drive their own learning. Often these particular children amaze me with their grit and creativity once they do get started, but they are initially crippled by their own sense of perfectionism or simply too many ideas that they cannot prune down. I've come to realise that it's important to acknowledge and explore the various reasons that students have for not jumping aboard, and provide structured choice for those that need it. If the students aren't running with the concept, there is little to be gained by forcing them before they are ready. Learning takes infinite forms, and as teachers we know that one size does not fit all.

Our usual Genius Hour process involves three clear phases, outlined in a class handout developed from a range of sources online and much trial and error. To the right is an outline of what each phase entails.

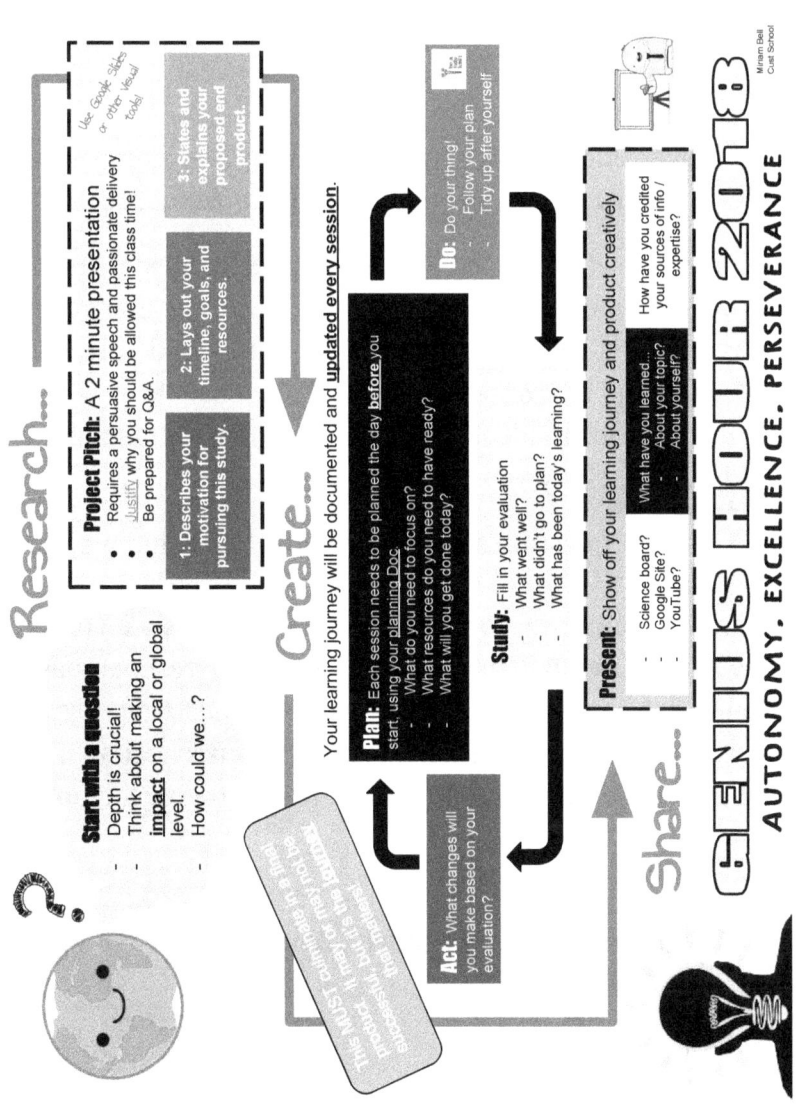

Chapter 11: A Rite of Passage

Phase 1: Research and Pitch

This is the most challenging bit, and by no means a one-lesson-wonder!

- Have children brainstorm what they love doing and how they could turn that into a purposeful project.

- Utilise reflective thinking strategies to decide which ideas would result in something awesome and achievable, and which are too narrow. Our class displays were full of cross-outs, arrows, and Post-Its as we came back to ideas, expanded on them, or dismissed them entirely.

- Use the question starters such as 'How could we...?'

When the concept is sorted, they need to convince you that it's worth pursuing. This can be a great tie-in to a persuasive language / speeches unit. No classroom has time for half-hearted or hare-brained schemes, so students need to prove that they have carefully considered the following factors:

- Costs.
- What resources are needed? Where are they coming from?
- Time management.

- What their learning will actually look like during Genius Hour.

- How they might use their learning to make a difference

As the teacher, you hold the veto card. Don't be afraid to use it. Ask hard questions and encourage the same from your students. Our 'Shark Tank' model usually has a number of classmates watching, and a presentation using Slides or some other presentation tool that is designed to convince us of the project's value. Over time, the students tend to drive the Q&A, and they are generally very good at giving and receiving feedback gracefully. This may be an area that you develop over time, depending on your particular class climate.

Phase 2: Create

During this phase, the classroom will probably be a bomb-site, and initially you may find yourself dashing from one crisis to another!

- Timetable workshops for specific skills (eg video editing, sawing etc) that need tuition. Ask your community for help if you're out of your depth.

- Allow children the space to solve their own problems. When you must intervene, use questioning strategies to lead them to their own solutions.

- Blogging is a great way to keep motivation levels high and to keep students accountable. They need to reflect on each session, recording progress and setbacks, and plan for the next week. This serves as a formative assessment tool, and the 'comment' function enables children to give their peers purposeful feedback. We have also used Hapara Workspace and Google Docs successfully to manage this essential part of the process.

Phase 3: Present

There needs to be an audience to celebrate the fabulous learning that has taken place; to inspire us by demonstrating and reflecting on what they had learned, both in their field of study and about themselves / the world. This also provides an avenue to teach and practice appropriate acknowledgement of sources. For us, sometimes this involved the children presenting their final products in the form of a TED talk, or website. We have also had class open days, or created visual displays that other classes and parents could interact with via the school office or hall.

Assessment

Despite good intentions, my carefully constructed 'Genius Hour' rubrics, assessment criteria and tick charts were ultimately binned, because they simply couldn't stand up to the scope and breadth of what the children were actually learning. This is real-life learning and it is much easier to reflect on after the fact, than predict in advance. Our focus throughout was developing 'Autonomy, Excellence, and Perseverance'. These attributes became the baseline that we returned to and unpacked, week after week. Some students need direct feedback that they weren't meeting these standards that we had set as a class.

The final products of this journey in our class continue to be many and varied. Some are simply outstanding. Some are not. A few never get off the ground at all. But all students are required to reflect on this, and all take responsibility for their own learning journey, regardless of the outcomes. The true power in Genius Hour lies in the fact that learning always evolves and leads to something else, and the limits are really only what we place on ourselves and our students.

Miriam Bell teaches Year 7-8 at Cust School, 20 minutes North of Christchurch. She has always enjoyed injecting creativity into the classroom, building on a baseline focus of core skill acquisition across the curriculum. When not teaching, she can be found spending time with her husband and 3 children, and whittling away endless hours on their lifestyle block. She also runs (quite slowly) and reads a lot of trashy fiction. Miriam can be contacted at

Miriam.bell@cust.school.nz

CHAPTER TWELVE

A Bigger Impact
Rachel O'Connell

An integral part of our process is for students to consider who is going to benefit from their Genius Hour project. Initially for many students it is simply themselves as they acquire new skills and knowledge. However, I do strongly encourage them to consider how others might benefit from their Genius Hour project too and how they can contribute as global citizens. For example, one child who wanted to learn how to sew, made library book bags to give away to other students within the school. Students love it when they realise that they can have an impact on others. Another group who wanted to develop their ukulele playing skills, then went and visited a local rest home and played for the elderly and performed at our end of year school prizegiving - they had purpose!

The model below has been used in my class (with permission from Anthony Speranza) and allows students to consider the world beyond themselves.

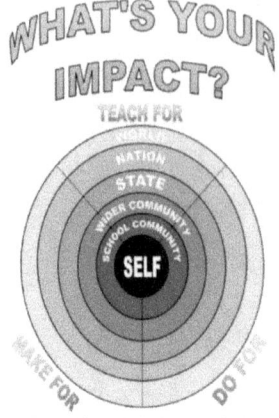

Before you begin, consider...

Who is going to benefit from your Genius Hour project?

Try to be as far-reaching as possible!

How will YOU have a positive impact on OTHERS?

Because of this focus, many of our Genius Hour projects have had a positive impact on our school community and into the wider community. Examples of these include:

Designing and building of scooter ramps for the school.

We are a rural school who used to have a 'wheels day' about once a term, encouraging students to bring bikes and scooters on that one day. As a result of three students designing and building a range of different scooter ramps, we are now an active 'scooter school' with a large percentage of our students scootering daily - for many students their scooters and helmets live at school permanently and only go home occasionally (this also led to another project involving the building of scooter stands). It is wonderful to see the older students teaching the younger students 'tricks' and helping them to refine their skills. Yes, there have been more band aids required in the medical room, but this has provided another opportunity for students to learn about pushing their limits.

Planning and running a community event - Trail Bike Ride.

One Genius Hour group took two terms to plan for and then run an inaugural trail bike ride on property in our local South Otago area. They took charge of the whole process, including contacting landowners, mapping out the course, Health and Safety plan, contacting an insurance company, sorting the PTA to provide lunch, safety briefing to all riders on the day... There was much to be learnt from this process and the best part was the day itself. Motorbike enthusiasts from the wider Otago region benefited from this event, as they had access to private farm land to explore. In addition, this Genius Hour group raised $1200 which they donated to our local pool to put towards a large slide (in turn continuing to benefit our whole community).

The trail bike ride organisers

Healthy drinks for school events: one project involved students investigating how to create healthy drinks that still taste good. They invented 'Smoocies' (a combination of smoothies and juices) which they then sold at our school disco as an alternative to fizzy drinks. These were very popular, tasted great and were a much healthier option for students.

Music performances: following their passion for music, one group further developed their ukulele playing skills. At the conclusion of their Genius Hour project, they approached a local rest home and visited to perform for the elderly. This group also performed at our end of year school production and were tutors to other students within the school during class ukulele sessions.

Planning and running a community event - Water Slide.

Another Genius Hour group wanted to provide something fun for the whole community to end the 2018 school year. They planned for, organised and ran a community water slide event one summer afternoon/evening. This was a huge success, with an impressive 100m water slide running downhill on a local farm. This was not a fundraiser, but an opportunity for some 'fun' for the community. The group learnt a great deal about organising, advertising, health and safety and the effort that goes in to running a successful event.

School checkerboard: realising that not all students are keen on taking part in physical activities during break times, one GH group surveyed the students to find out what other options they might like around our school to make break times more fun for everyone. After collating the results of their survey, they set about designing, measuring and painting a checkerboard on concrete outside. This is now used by students to play checkers during morning tea and lunchtimes. The students now have the aim of fundraising to purchase some large chess pieces in the immediate future.

Tables from recycled wooden pallets: many of the best projects stem from a need, problem or issue. One that we had at our school was that there weren't enough outdoor picnic tables for all of the students to sit at for lunch or if they chose to work outside. This led to one group designing and creating their own by recycling wooden pallets. They built two which are very sturdy and in daily use at our school.

Fundraising for the children's ward of Dunedin Hospital: while I prefer to steer clear of fundraisers, one group really wanted to do something positive for children who end up in hospital. So they organised and ran a number of fundraising events at school, such as a disco and mufti day. They contacted the hospital and found out what sort of items would be useful to help stimulate and entertain children who need to spend time in hospital. The highlight for this group was delivering their goodies to the hospital and seeing the delight on the faces of the children.

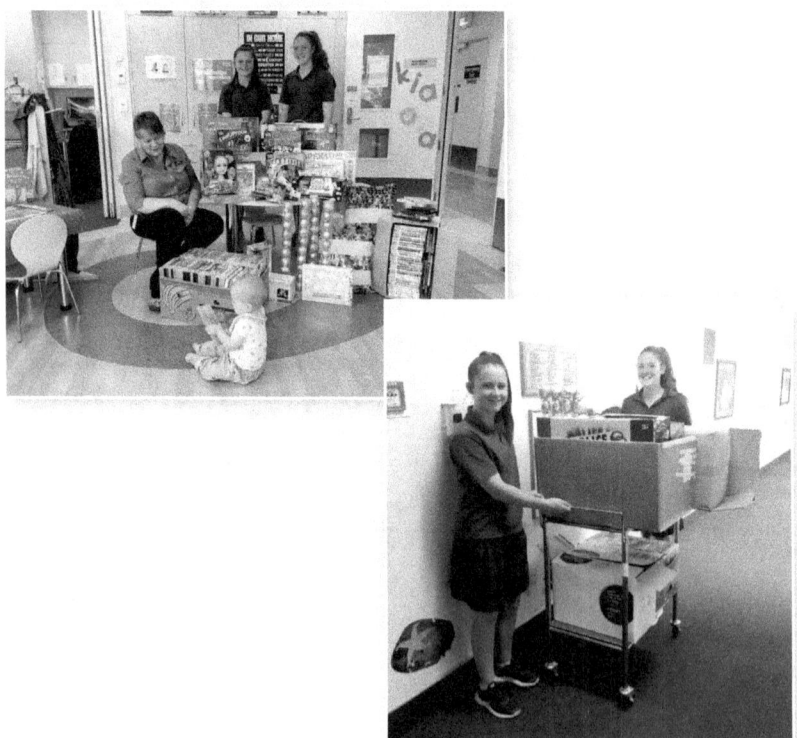

Encouraging Community Involvement

Right from the planning/ proposal stage I encourage students to think about who can mentor or support them with their Genius Hour project. At times they may need pointing in the direction

of an 'expert' or 'mentor', but the students must make contact themselves and arrange a suitable time to meet up. The meeting could be at school, via a Skype or Google Hangout, a phone call or even a visit from the students to the mentor.

Students are supported throughout this process, with examples of phone call scripts or emails provided as scaffolds. No phone calls are made or emails sent until the teacher has given approval, upon viewing the telephone script or email (this is from past experience, where students were phoning people 'willy-nilly').

Our students are fortunate that they have had very positive involvement and support from the wider community throughout their various Genius Hour projects.

A highlight for the community members involved is being invited back to the presentation of the Genius Hour projects during Week 10.

Top Tips

- Research yourself and be clear of 'your' process - if you are clear then the students will be confident too

- Allow plenty of time during the ideation and question stages - a bit of hand holding and then release. If the leading question is not deep the whole project suffers. If the question is right it sets the lens for what might come.

- Encourage group Genius Hour projects - this allows you to give time to support each project. Too many individual projects and you are stretched. Also, it provides the perfect opportunity for students to develop effective collaboration skills.

- Steer clear of fundraisers!

- Seek extra adult help for the first couple of sessions - our Principal steps in and supports until the question is developed, as this is the time when we are very busy, prompting and challenging each group to think deeply.

- Create a deadline for students and stick to it!

- Guide the students to seek outside mentors to support them

- Check in regularly with each group - touch base with where they are at and what they need to do next. Having a system for monitoring/recording/keeping track of each group as you conference with them works well.

- Failure for students is important - value it *e.g. learning to choose the right people to work with, time management, getting the driving question succinct....* Often the least successful outcomes produce the greatest learning opportunities.

- Encourage students to work on developing their presentation to the class throughout the Genius Hour time frame, not just at the end.

- Adapt! No two Genius Hours should be the same - my templates for students have changed every year as I refine the process.

- Don't be frightened to let go of the reins

- Connect with other teachers - the Genius Hour/20% NZ Facebook page is a great place to start, as is Twitter and Pinterest.

- Take time to celebrate

Rachel O'Connell is an experienced classroom practitioner, currently teaching Year 5-8 students at Clutha Valley School in South Otago. She loves students driving their own learning and finds Genius Hour to be the perfect vehicle for student agency. A lifelong learner, Rachel particularly enjoys developing further digital technologies skills. When not teaching, she loves to spend time exploring the outdoors with her husband and twin sons.

Twitter - @rachoconnell1

CHAPTER THIRTEEN

A Whole Class Project
Nik Edwards

Kids teaching kids? It was a simple plan. I was lucky to be working in Tawa School when Anne Maree Breen was Principal. She employed me to run the experimental City School where I ran my class from an old central city classroom.

The pupils and I spent our days actually in the city and used city locations and situations as our learning centres. We studied real life topics in real life situations and extended our experiences by introducing experts in the city to talk to us.

We took over the first floor of the Old St George hotel which meant we could walk out into the city and were conveniently situated for our frequent visitors.

Seventeen pupils were armed with Apple laptops - cutting edge at the time and each pair were allocated a mobile phone and a research question and tasks, each with a Wellington business.

The pupils would devise their own programmes and would work with a specific business. Some of these projects included Weta Workshop – creative development in the film industry, the Central Library, a local bakery, and Whitcoulls book store. After a particularly interesting speaker who addressed our group on the subject of endangered animals, which he illustrated with shredded snake skins, ivory and other banned items, the pupils suggested that the rest of the school should have the opportunity to share in some of their adventures. This idea was reinforced after a another interesting workshop with a customs officer.

From here the idea of running a Kids Conference was born.

A Kids Conference is Born

Find a venue said our Principal. And so we did. The children hunted the streets of Wellington and found Westpac Stadium.

Students wanted to share their ideas to see if others liked the concept and they went to a local school to sound out their students. They were keen.

Next step was sponsorship and the students presented in front of the Community Trust of Wellington committee. They explained the concept – a conference for kids run by kids and provided an approximate budget. During the presentation, one student fumbled and bumbled – then picked himself up and carried on. These are the real life moments you never forgot as a teacher. I was so proud. The members were impressed and agreed to be a major sponsor.

Students made lists of expert presenters and contacted them via fax and email. Students worked on advertising, catering, contacting schools, programming, entertainment, ticket sales – it was full on!

The conference opened with a haka performance followed by two and a half days of workshops. Two hundred of Wellington's business people, artists, writers, academics, sportsmen and scientists. The students would select their own programmes for the day choosing which workshop they would attend.

Experts included scientists in different fields, astrologists, meteorologists, palaeontologists, zoologists, virologists, mathematicians, doctors, sports doctors, lawyers, armed services (army, navy, airforce), nurses, physiotherapists, customs, marine biologists, musicians, entrepreneurs, sports administrators, engineers, life coaches, builders, electricians, nutritionists, triathletes, martial arts, calligraphy, cake decorators, ecologists, also some really brilliant teachers from all over New Zealand (drama, dance, art, music and mathematics).

From years five to year eight they came from all over the country. We held twenty three workshops every fifty minutes for two and a half days.

The conference was so successful it ran for 7 years.

In the final year the conference saw over five hundred students and two hundred experts. We also had a few students who ran their own workshops. There were several buses transporting attendees around the city and video conferences sessions to include others schools and activities.

Our wonderful guests included Lynda Hallinan (writer & editor), Jeff Kennedy (coffee legend), Dinah Priestly (artist & actress), Jim Anderton & Peter Dunne (members of Parliament), Danyon Loader (double Olympian gold medallist swimmer) and many more.

One of the special moments was having a group of kids board the HMAS Melbourne, an Australian frigate, and have a tour on board as the ship pulled in to the Overseas Terminal.

Getting Out and About included Workshops in cake baking, drama coaching, art (botanic gardens) cartooning, Trips to Logan Brown restaurant (Celebrity Chef), Zealandia

(Wildlife Sanctuary), Te Papa (National Museum), Victoria University. Anywhere we could send kids in buses we did!

We had some great speakers including a number of Ministers and notable sports people. Our Prime Minister at the time Helen Clarke turned up a couple of times over the years and to her credit stuck around for a while and answers many questions.

Other notable dignitaries included champion runner, Melissa Moon, Coast to Coast champion Steve Gurney (adventure racer), Footballer of the Century Wynton Rufer, Richard Taylor took time out of a busy Weta Workshop (special effects and props for television and film) schedule to come in and Karen Boyes was a keynote at most of them.

There were so many people who contributed to the conference in so many ways. They volunteered their time, their skills and sometimes their equipment.

Learning Through Challenges

There were surprisingly few glitches over the years. One was a group of cricket enthusiasts whose speaker failed to turn up found themselves making elaborate sparkly animal masks.

Another was when the catering was not what was promised. Students were annoyed about this and called a meeting with the catering company to point out the differences between what was promised and delivered. It was a great opportunity for self-advocacy. The company agreed with the students disappointment and dropped the charges significantly.

Some of the Highlights

One great aspect was kids from different schools mixing at the conference. Each Learning Station had mixed groups of students from different schools and ages.

My favourite presentation from the Antarctic Research Victoria University. Kids got to dress up in real gear and look at how to survive in such harsh environment.

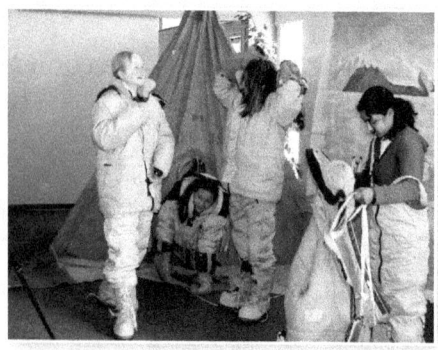

Geological studies with another workshop from Victoria University.

Kids learning to fly helicopters, fighter planes and Jumbo jets. This was before the age of flight simulators became popular.

Nik Edwards is a teacher an with an M.Ed. (Victoria University) who has taught all over New Zealand and overseas. He has run conferences for kids in Auckland, Rotorua, Christchurch and Wellington. He created Kids Conference from a City Class project at based at Tawa School in Wellington in 2001. Kids Conference ran in Wellington for seven years until 2008. Over 4000 students and 1400 experts experienced this unique project.

Nik can be contacted at nikedwards1@gmail.com

CHAPTER FOURTEEN

Beyond The Basics
Kyle Hattie

Genius Hour, Passion Projects, Project Based Learning, iExplore, Break Through; there are a lot of different ways of saying it but they all have the same idea, learners using their passions, strengths and curiosities to drive their learning. I am a Year 4, 5 and 6 teacher with 56 students in an Innovative Learning Environment, that I share with one other teacher. Over the last 5 years we have been exploring and learning about how to move the students beyond the surface ideas and developing vocabulary and knowledge to them forming relations between these ideas, exploring problems, working with open ideas, and transferring their understanding to new contexts and problems.

I have implemented passion projects with learners, from new entrants all the way to intermediate age. This was sparked due to a workshop I attended at all about Genius Hour. When the school I was working at started to develop their own way of doing Genius Hour I was determined to make this the best part of a learners week and get the most learning out of it I could. I have seen both successful and unsuccessful projects over the years, but what I have noticed is that the motivation, resilience, initiative and deep thinking that the learners are developing are the most out of any subject I teach.

In my experience with Genius Hour I see three important keys to success; The purpose, the learning process, and the teachers vs. students role in the learning. In this chapter I will be referring to Genius Hour as Break Through, because at Stonefields Primary School in Auckland, where I currently teach, we have developed our own way of doing this type of learning that works for our context and learners.

The Purpose

When you think about Genius Hour, ask yourself 'Why am I doing this?' With all the pressures of to cover so much of the curriculum throughout a year to ensure you are getting at least 12 months gain for 12 months input, this question is often asked? If you want your learners to be sure of the purpose and to maximise their learning then you need, as the teacher, to know the purpose of the Break Through. As do the students. The purpose of what you are doing needs to be at the forefront of any project. American motivator and writer Simon Sinek's idea of 'The Golden Circle' puts the "why" at the centre of the circle.

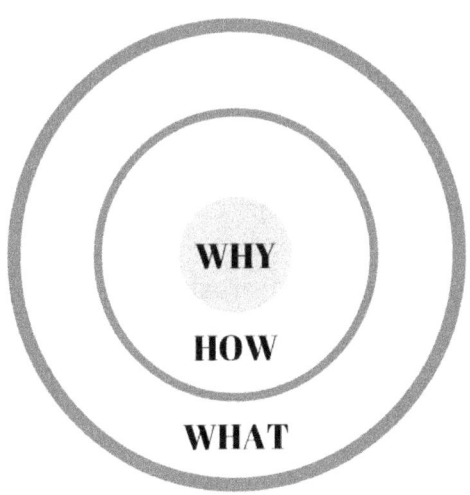

Sinek, in his book *Start with Why* (2009), talks about big business and noted that every company knows what they do. They can explain how they do it but when asked the question why to do they do it, many fail to answer. When you have a three-year old, their most common question is Why? By age 8, too often they default to "What" (although as adolescents they come back to Why not?). The purposes of education are to know the what, understand the how, and ponder on the why. Ryle (1948) made this important distinction between "knowing what" and "knowing how" – we may know what it takes to ride a bike but maybe not how – to which there is the higher question – Why ride this bike (and this destination often leads to wanting to know more about the knowing what and knowing how. This is too often the problem with most Genius Hour projects, that I have experienced or seen, the learners can tell exactly what they are doing, and sometimes even how they are doing. They see the 'what' as the purpose but must also understand the 'why'.

Take the following scenario for example "(this is a real scenario from a year 5 student):

> Teacher "What is your break through idea?" Year 5 student "I am going to 3D print a house."
>
> Teacher "that sounds fun, what learning are you going to take from this?"
>
> Year 5 Student "I will learn how to 3D print a house"

From this interaction about the learner's project you can see that they have really thought about what they want to do. When questioned about the purpose they were very literal, but it is still the 'what'. Yes, the student may have learnt how to use a new tool but he is limiting the potential of the project. As a teacher I can see how much learning there is in what he wanted to do. I can see lessons that involve measurement, design thinking, scale, research about architecture through different countries, and spatial literacy. But the learner does not see that—he sees a 3D printer. As teachers, we need to see and communicate the "Why" behind the project. We need to encourage the learners to think beyond 'what' they want to do, 'what' could they make or 'what' may be fun, and more into 'why' am I learning this, and 'why' is this going to help me. The learner in the scenario could be moving towards: "I want to learn about architecture and use the 3D printer to showcase my design principles". This will allow him to get higher and deeper levels learning out of passion hour and have a richer experience. It is worth working with the students to help them articulate the "why" of the project, and maybe turn these into co-constructed success criteria that can then help structure the 'what' of the project, and also provide a benchmark to evaluate the 'how' in terms of progress to these goals.

Take the following projects that I have had learners want to pursue: Art, Science, Minecraft, Paper airplanes, Animals, Sports, and Dance. All are definitely great topics to teach but they may not work as great topics or lead to worthwhile Break through or Genius Hour projects. They are great topics that may motivate students to pursue but they are the what, not the why. The principles are to take these 'what's' and attach them to a purpose to then become a 'why' for example:

- Art - learning to share ideas and messages through Art. Take Banksy, for example, the street artist that takes political messages to make people question society. This a worthy cause. The why can relate more to the ideas of how Banksy uses inferencing, symbolism, sharing messages and different art styles to convey his message.

- Sport - I want to organise a soccer tournament and teach fair play because too many people are cheating in our games and argue. The 'why' behind this developing principle of mutual respect through organisational skills, procedural writing to create the rules and aims, writing a proposal to the principal to get the tournament in school time, and appropriate advertising.

Enabling the Purpose

These examples show the why behind what the learners are wanting to do. Like Sinek's model, we need to encourage the learners to start with the 'Why'. To assist in enabling the learners to focus on the why or purpose of the Genius Hour, is to put some constraints around the ideas is a good way of starting? Fig. 1 suggests that there are three stages of discussing these constraints.

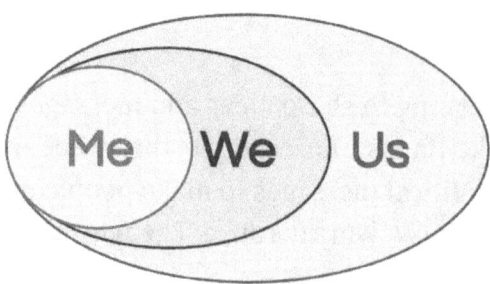

Learners often start at the Me stage. What is going to benefit me? What is a problem that I have to solve? You can ask the student by posing the question "What problem are you trying to fix?" or "What will benefit you and why?" in order to encourage the learners to think more about the purpose of the project.

The next stage is the 'We' and this is where they start thinking not only about what will help them but more about how others can help them and they can help others. This could include the community, school, family, whanau, or a group of friends.

If they are struggling with a focus of their project, then a good place to start is to have the learners walk around the school to try to find problems. A colleague of mine did this with her year 2 learning hub and they decided that there was not enough shade out the back of their learning hub for them to use the space. This ended up with a pitch to the Board of Trustees to fund a shade sail (which was successful!). Looking for purposes that will benefit the group will encourage the learners to think wider than just themselves.

The last stage is the 'Us' and this where we invoke global thinking. Not just you and your community but the world as a whole. This is the blue sky thinking about what will help the country or world thinking. Take the UN global goals as a provocation.

If learners can use these as a provocation then they are really thinking about real and relevant learning. It is not necessary that the learners need to think globally all the time but learners understanding the 'why' behind what they are doing will allow them to take more learning from the project; and there are many Whys in these development goals. If the learners can articulate why, how and what they are doing then they will get more out of the project. So think about the 'why', what is our purpose? A major role as the teacher is to help the students become clear about the 'why'.

High Expectations for Purposes

Developing high expectations for the students and have the right balance of not too easy, not too hard challenging success criteria are necessarily early steps to success. Consider the Flea in the Jar experiment. In this experiment a scientist put a flea in a jar and kept the lid off. Because the flea can jump more than 100 times it body height, it had no problem jumping out of the jar. Then the flea was placed in the jar again but the scientist put the lid on the jar. The flea now jumped and hit the lid. After a few jumps the flea adapted how it was jumping and only jumped high enough so that it did not hit the jar lid. After a while the scientist took the lid off and the flea had adapted and still jumped the same reduced (just below the lid) height so was unable to get out of the jar. This experiment showed that putting limitations on the flea made the flea adapt and change.

As teachers if we have low expectations of the learners then we are stopping them to reach their potential. Are we putting a lid on students learning by our expectations of Break Through or Genius Hour projects?

Having a structure for learning and giving the learners freedom to explore, fail, relearn, and think bigger than we can imagine, learners are more likely to reach the true potential of their project.

The Learning Process

From the beginning of my schooling, as a student in school, I always found learning very difficult. I was the student in the back of the class saying the right things and looking busy, but inside I was confused. I wanted to learn and I have always enjoyed finding out about new things. But as a student I struggled and this continued throughout high school and university. I soon learnt to look busy, and avoid being asked the tough questions.

Now as a teacher and having taught in many different contexts and year levels, I look back on my education and wish I could go back in time with what I know now and do it again. I put this down to the Learning Process.

I know now that it helps up front and during the lessons to have a pathway, a model, a visible journey of my learning, exemplars of the thinking required – and this has been vital to my teaching and subsequently to the success of the learners. Learners knowing where they are in the learning, what the next step is, know how to seek and interpret feedback, and have multiple (e.g., 2-3) different thinking strategies has unlocked so much of the unknown for learners. When I was at school I did what I was told and then asked for the next step.

When we look at Genius Hour , it is important for learners to first and foremost understand what the process of learning is; be confident about failing and making mistakes; know how to seek and interpret feedback; understand how to seek advice from peers or teachers about the next steps; know what to do when these best next steps turn out to not so successful.

Imagine two students conferencing with the teacher about their project.

> Student 1: My break through project is reducing the sense of loneliness and enhancing the sense of belonging in this school. I want to build a seat for the school. A bench for students to sit on when they are feeling lonely or want someone to play with and when people see this they will know and ask them to play. It's a buddy bench.
>
> Teacher: That's a great idea. What are you going to need to do to make sure this happens? What are you next steps?
>
> Student 1: Build it.
>
> Teacher: Ok. How?
>
> Student 1: Oh, just nail it together.
>
> Teacher: Where you going to get the Material?
>
> Student 1: Um, I'm not sure.
>
> Student 2: Can you do that for us Mr. Hattie, or maybe we could ask our parents for help here.

Consider the scenario. This involves a group of learners with a great idea. They really knew the why behind their project.

But when it came to the how they were stumped. Like Sinek's Golden Circle Model they knew they had to start at the why. But when you move to the next circle, How, they were not sure. This has been the same with many of the Break Through and other Passion led projects that I have encountered over the years. Learners become so excited and invested in the idea, the why, and are less able to see the what or process. Right now, however, we are fortunate that there are many debates and models about the learning process. Stonefields School, where I work currently, have developed their own learning process model and it is deliberately taught across everything we teach and create at every year level in the school.

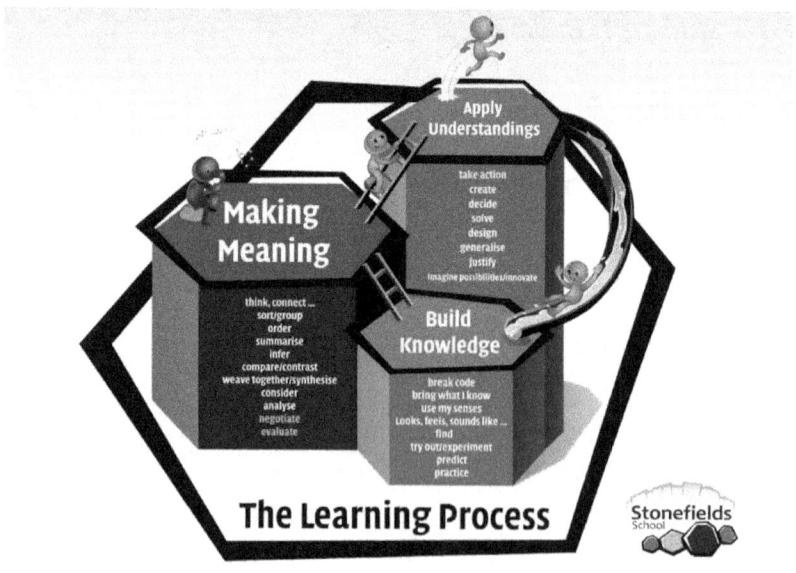

This process was developed intentionally based on sound research and debates among the staff at Stonefields. It takes ideas from research such as the Bloom (2000) and SOLO (Biggs & Collis, 1982) taxonomy, just to name a few, and combines it with thinking of the staff as how they see learning. Each section has different learning verbs attached to it, so the learners has a language of learning. This allows a common narrative or shared language of learning, allows students to grow in their learning building this common narrative from year to year, from class to class.

The three phases lead to an evolving fluid process.

Build Knowledge is where learners are finding, predicting, trying out and experimenting about the context in which they are learning. The purpose is to find out what the learners already know, what questions they have about the context, or just immerse themselves in the context. From this phase the learners will find out what is hard, what they can and cannot do, and what they might need help with. At this phase, there needs to be opportunities to build vocabulary, ideas, brainstorm and think about what might work or not.

Make Meaning follows. In this phase you are taking what you know and building on it with a deeper understanding or developing cognitive complexity. If you take the context of a baking soda and vinegar rocket, in Making Meaning you can analyse the resolutes of what happens when you mix the two ingredients. You can organise data and learning about why the combination of the ingredients makes a chemical reaction. This is building on new information and knowing how to sort your understanding to start to transfer the knowledge. At this phase there is intentional building of relations between the ideas developing during the Build Knowledge phase.

The third phase is **Apply Understanding**. In this phase you are taking the learning that you have done in each phase and combining it to apply it to various contexts. The learning about rockets, chemical reactions, releasing of gases needed to have a successful science experiment can now be applied to other areas. This is the transference of knowledge, deep thinking, and where the learning sticks. These three phases are not linear. You may have to jump between Build Knowledge and Make Meaning a few different times. You may have to go through the processes more than once. But what this gives learners is a framework or pathway from their idea to the various success criteria or not only knowing many ideas, but seeing relations between ideas, and transferring their new learning to new situations or contexts.

Teacher Control vs Learner Control

This is one of the ideas that I have discussed, argued and explored at great length with Genius Hour. Some teachers say that if the teacher is in control and pushing a direction than this will stifle the learners creativity, which can occur.

But on the other hand, if the teacher is not promoting a direction then nothing may get done and the learners may not take any learning deeply and it becomes a waste of learning potential. So what is the answer? I believe that both teacher and student have a vital role for the success of the project, and often it is matter of when. It is worth considering the various roles of the learner and the teacher.

The Learners role can include: ideas, motivation, planning/timeline, learning, and finding ways to improve outcomes. The teachers role can include: ensuring that the learners will be successful and there are clear success criteria about the Why of each project, ensuring that the learning involved is not too hard in which learners become disheartened and unmotivated, checking in to make sure that the timeline is being met, challenging thinking so that the learners are going beyond the surface level, and supporting when stuck

If you look at those roles you will see that there is much overlap in the roles. The major difference is that the learners are doing the learning and pushing themselves and the teacher is ensuring that they are learning and supporting the transition from surface to deep learning. At times the teacher may be in more control (e.g., at the outset to ensure Why foci) and at times the learners are in more control (e.g., in relating ideas and learning from failure).

The following scenario is one based off of a group of year 3 and 4 students.

Imagine a group of year 3 and 4 students who loved riding bikes. They could talk about it for hours and rode their bikes to school every day rain or shine. They decided that they would do their project on trying to create a place to ride bikes at school. They went through the Build knowledge phase and found out as much as they could about making ramps, pictures, videos, they even drew what it might look like. As a teacher I saw the potential of their idea. It was great for the community and they were so keen. I wanted to support and push the potential. I worked with them to have a major purpose of the project, which they enjoyed. But when we started talking about what might be involved, such as measurements, wood work, an investigation into whether the school would want their project, and asked whether it would be used by more than them, there were many doubts. The learners instantly thought, this is going to be too hard. They reverted to saying they just want to build a single ramp. The motivation was starting to be overshadowed by their confidence in their academic ability to plan, relate ideas, and transfer their knowledge to new contexts. But I told them I would help and in mathematics lessons and literacy lessons we can work together to support their learning. The students became so excited about the prospect of their passion project and that it could be a focus of their math lesson and reading lesson. The motivation and confidence instantly returned.

In this scenario we had learners who started out with a massive blue sky thinking idea. Then the reality of what they need to learn to be successful set in. This is where the teacher's role is vital. I could have been like the scientist in the Flea experiment where putting a lid on the jar says, "No that's too hard for you" and you need to change or at least reduce the expectations of their idea but I wanted them to be successful and we worked together. My role was the person who could teach them what they needed and their role was to take the knowledge and apply it in the time allocated for the project. Both of us worked towards their goal. In the end the learners did the work, pitched the idea to the board of trustees, and it was integrated into the long term plan for that school. The learners went far beyond the ideas, and worked at the higher levels of Learning processes, and their motivation to learn new knowledge was amazing. Thus, a fundamental role of the teachers is to maximize the probability that the learners attain the success criteria. This will mean us being in control in this respect and saying yes your idea can work or unfortunately no that idea will be too big or not achievable in the time. This is based on a deep knowledge of the students and setting that lid at the right height for them to achieve new, deep learning.

With so many learners, so many ideas, this may sound like a lot of work and organisation. This is why I organise Passion Projects in groups of students. This is why I spend time up front with the groups working on their Why, which often helps put boundaries around the possible. This is why we work out early what knowledge, resources, and help we need to get started. Having the learners come up with a pitch for their idea often means they have early buy-in to the project, and the seeking of any new knowledge. In developing the pitch, allows them to think about the learning involved and the do-ability of the idea. Below is an example of a process to begin the Passion Projects based on the TV Dragons Den. We gave them a deadline in which they had to pitch their idea to the "Dragon's den" and we either said yes or no or gave them something to think about and another chance to do their pitch. A constraint is that the pitch needs to relate to a higher level topic (e.g., "Our Future our World"), which was perfect for a Break Through or Genius Hour project. Below are some of the examples of the planning for this.

From the years of the exploring passion led learning like Genius Hour. I have found that you can make this process extremely enjoyable and to get the most out of it you need to put the ground work into it, and ensure it set to have maximum chances of success. I have found a lot of success by focusing the three key elements; The purpose, the learning process, and the teachers vs students roles in the learning. If you can set the Passion Project with these elements then students will be able to take the learning and transfer the skills into their Projects so as to be successful. The challenge is to incorporate and trial Passion Projects in your class. Whether or not you have done this type of learning or not before, the learners will thank you for it.

Kyle Hattie is a year 4/5/6 teacher working at Stonefields Primary School in an Innovative Learning Environment. He is passionate about bringing learners strength and world to life through teaching and learning. Genius Hour has been a big part of this over the last 5 years. When not teaching you can find Kyle with his wife and two girls exploring new places around Auckland.

Contact @KyleHattie on twitter.

APPENDIX ONE

More Driving Question Examples

- What can we do to slow down or prevent damage from climate change?
- How does the clock hands move on a clock?
- How do dolphins affect the ecosystems they live in?
- How can people with nothing be so happy?
- How might I learn to about the causes and preventions for diabetes?
- How might I teach someone how a thermos works?
- How might I learn some magic tricks?
- How might I learn how to become a master chef?

- How might I make people aware of the dangers of smoking and vaping?

- How might I learn how to create an 'app'?

More Examples of Genius Hour Projects at Clutha Valley School

- How might we be able to use old clothes to create new outfits?

- How might I educate people that parrots make great pets?

- How might I develop younger children's basketball skills?

- How might we create a 3D scale model of our dream house to teach others about construction?

- How can we raise awareness about animal abuse?

- How might we reduce possums by making a possum trap out of household items?

- How might we create a billy cart that everyone will enjoy going on?

- How might we persuade people that Minecraft involves maths?

- How might we learn and teach others sign language to support those with hearing impairments?

- How might we be able to make kids and families less fortunate than us enjoy Christmas more?
- How might we create a way to show others different hairstyles?
- How might we make outside furniture out of recycled pallets?
- How might we teach people about the benefits of gaming?
- How might we improve our playground with fun bright colours?
- How might we create a movie with a good message?
- How might I make soap that is good for eczema, that the world will benefit from?
- How can we learn a new skill like sewing and help the hospital at the same time?
- How might I create awareness of endangered animal species?
- How might we make a boat out of everyday materials?
- How might I teach others about the importance of coding and how to code?
- How might I create awareness about diabetes and find out about healthy food options for diabetics?

- How might we make household items that don't have harmful chemicals in them?

- How might we create a song on the ukulele that will change people's minds about life?

- How might we raise poultry within a tight budget?

- How might we create a sport to interest and entertain both boys and girls while keeping them fit?

Bibliography

Ashby, Simon. (2017) *Utilising your students' passions through 'Genius Hour'* Teachers Matter Magazine, Issue 31. Pages 18-19. New Zealand

Bell, Miriam. (2017) *Genius Hour: Allow your students to follow their passions.* Teachers Matter Magazine, Issue 30, pages 20-21. New Zealand

Boyes, Karen Tui. (2001) *Creating An Effective Learning Environment.* Spectrum Education. New Zealand

Boyes, Karen Tui. (2018) *Study Smart – Your Essential Guide To Passing Exams.* Spectrum Education. New Zealand

Boyes, Karen Tui & Watts, Graham. (2009) *Developing Habits of Mind in Elementary Schools:* An ASCD Action Tool. ASCD, USA

Boyes, Karen Tui & Watts, Graham. (2009) *Developing Habits of Mind in Secondary Schools:* An ASCD Action Tool. ASCD, USA

Brookhouser Kevin (2012) *20% Project: Bad Idea Factory.* kevinbrookhouser.com

Brown, Brené. (2015) *Rising Strong.* Random House, New York

Costa, Arthur & Kallick, Bena (2008) *Learning and Leading with Habits of Mind : 16 Essential Characteristics for Success.* ASCD, USA

Covey, Stephen R. Merrill, Roger, Merrill, Rebecca (1996) *First Things First.* Prentice Hall

Crouch, Kim. (2017) *Genius Hour and Inquiry-Based Learning.* englishonmy.com

Davis, Rebecca. (2018) *Genius Hour Journal for Students.* Differentiated Teaching

Dooly, Renee. *Awakening Genius Hour in your classroom.* theteacherbag.com

Dweck, Carol. (2006) *Mindset: The New Psychology of Success.* Random House

Kallick, Bena & Zmunda, Alison (2016) *Students at the Center: Personalized Learning with Habits of Mind.* ASCD

Jackson, Karen. *Genius Hour.* applejacksteacher.com

Juliani, A.J. *5 Reasons To Try Genius Hour Before The End Of The School Year.* ajjuliani.com

Juliani, A.J. (2014) *Inquiry & Innovation in the Classroom: Using Genius Hour, 20% Time, and PBL to Drive Student Success.* Routledge

Nottingham, James. (2017) *The Learning Challenge.* Corwin

Maiers, Angela, (2016) *Liberating Genius.* Lulu.com

Pink, Daniel (2009) *'Drive – The Surprising Truth About What Motivates Us.'* Riverhead Books, New York.

Shelley. *Genius Hour in the Primary Classroom.* Thewritestuffteaching.com

Subramanian, Sushma. (2013) *Google Took Its 20% Back, But Other Companies Are Making Employee Side Projects Work For Them.* fastcompany.com

Professional Development Options with Karen Tui Boyes

Award winning international educator Karen Tui Boyes is available to present to and work with Teachers, Students and Parents. Below are some options for you to be able to access Karen's expertise and knowledge to assist you in raising achievement and preparing students for the world ahead. All PLD is personalised to the needs of your students, teachers & goals of the school/conference or organisation.

Ways you might engage Karen to work with Teachers, Students & Parents...

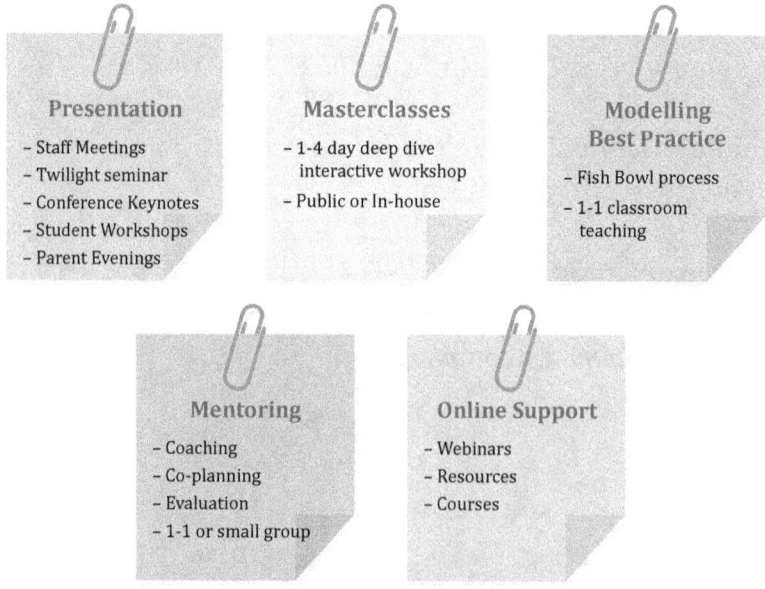

Presentation
- Staff Meetings
- Twilight seminar
- Conference Keynotes
- Student Workshops
- Parent Evenings

Masterclasses
- 1-4 day deep dive interactive workshop
- Public or In-house

Modelling Best Practice
- Fish Bowl process
- 1-1 classroom teaching

Mentoring
- Coaching
- Co-planning
- Evaluation
- 1-1 or small group

Online Support
- Webinars
- Resources
- Courses

Topics include:

For more information please go to:
www.spectrumeducation.com/pld-kahui-ako

Stay in Touch with Karen

To subscribe to Karen's updates and articles please go to www.spectrumeducation.com or email the Spectrum Office info@spectrumeducation.com

To read Karen's latest articles go to:
www.karentuiboyes.com/blog

Find out about events Spectrum Education & Karen is hosting go to: www.spectrumeducation.com/events

To discuss your PLD needs please contact the Spectrum Education office on info@spectrumeducation.com or call us and leave a message on +64 4 528 9969

You can email Karen direct at
karen@spectrumeducation.com

Gratitude & Thanks

This book has been a work of love, passion, dedication and hard work! Hours of silent solitude of focus, huge 'do to' lists and self-discipline! It is easy to talk about writing a book, doing it is a whole different story! I'm grateful that the stars and angels aligned for this to become a reality.

As always, a book like this could not happen without a team of people in the background – and I would like to acknowledge them.

I stand on the shoulders of giants and am so blessed to have these people who are mentors and friends who continue to inspire me daily. These include, Professor Art Costa, Dr Bena Kallick, Christopher Evans, Tony Ryan, Dr Rich Allen and Dr William Sommers. Your teachings have contributed to this book in both small and big ways. Thanks.

Gratitude must go to the use of the kitchen tables in Marion Miller and Michelle Boyde's homes. Thanks for allowing me to extend my stay in your homes and giving me the space and freedom to just write. It made all the difference.

At the conception of this book idea I immediately contacted five teachers who I knew were doing amazing Genius Hour work in their classrooms and asked them to contribute. All said yes and worked under a tight time frame to get me their chapter. Simon Ashby, Miriam Bell, Rachel O'Connell, Nik Edwards and Kyle Hattie, thanks for sharing your practical applications as well and your highs and lows, the reality of implementing Genius Hour in the classroom. You have deepened the readers knowledge and understanding. Thank you.

Thanks also goes to the teachers in classrooms all over the world, ones I have met, worked with and learned from, those I am yet to meet. Thanks for all you do to inspire the youth of today. Every day, in some way, you make every other profession possible. I am in awe of the work you do and hope this book inspires you to give Genius Hour a whirl in your classroom.

To the current and past team at Spectrum, thanks and gratitude for all the help, advice, feedback and new learning and insights. You are an awesome group of people, focused on our goal of being At The Heart of Teaching and Learning. Thanks for believing in my vision and keeping everything ticking while I wrote.

To Jessica Youmans for your editing work on the manuscript and to Megan Gallagher, for being an awesome colleague, friend, confidant and providing escapism when I was in the midst of writing. Our day in Oamaru refreshed and revived me to keep going!

To my very own rainbows and sunshine, my geniuses, Hamish and Sasha. Your school journeys and experiences have both frustrated and inspired me to want to make all students educational ventures beneficial, meaningful and full of profound learning. I'm grateful for who you are and all you do.

My final gratitude & love goes to Denny MacArthur – who has played many roles in the making of this book – spouse, friend, fan, editor and most importantly cook and bottle washer! With you by my side, everything is possible!

www.ingramcontent.com/pod-product-compliance
Lightning Source LLC
Chambersburg PA
CBHW050634300426
44112CB00012B/1800